Diary of Dr. Rosetta Hall
1890

Volume 1

Rosetta Sherwood Hall

En route from Liberty,
New York to Seoul,
Korea via San Francisco

Preface

Dr. Rosetta Sherwood Hall was born in 1865 in Liberty, New York, the daughter of a well-to-do Christian farming family. She obtained a teacher's certificate at the age of sixteen, and after teaching at local schools for a few years, was sent in 1890 to the remote far eastern land of Korea to devote her life to medicine and missionary work under the auspices of the Woman's Medical Missionary Society of the Methodist Episcopal Church. She would go on to serve as a medical missionary there for forty-three years.

For hundreds of years, Korea had observed the 내외법 *Nae Wae Beop*, a Confucian law stipulating the strict segregation of gender. This law had restricted women's access to formal education, professional training, political representation, and movement in the public sphere. Missionaries like Dr. Rosetta Hall dedicated themselves not only to serving women who did not have access to proper medical care, but also to widely expanding these women's social opportunities and renewing their sense of self-esteem. With the heart of Christ, Dr. Rosetta Hall exercised love and compassion on Korea's underprivileged.

Her significant achievements include adapting Braille into Korean script, which inaugurated a formalized education system for Korea's blind and deaf. She trained many girls and young women in the medical profession, giving them the knowledge and agency to care for their own people.

At the time of appointment, she was supposed to have served a five-year term in the field as a single missionary. Two years into her term, she married Rev. William James Hall, M.D., whom she met in the slums of New York City while they were working as medical missionaries there. Until Rev. Hall's tragic death by typhus fever in November 1894, they worked in Seoul, started work in Pyongyang, and began raising a newborn son, Sherwood.

After burying her beloved husband, Rosetta returned to New York with her infant son and a daughter in her womb. While in the States, she furthered the work she undertook in Korea. She oversaw the education of Esther Pak Kim, Korea's first female doctor of medicine, who received her M.D. degree in 1900 at the Baltimore Woman's Medical College; she raised funds and established the Hall Memorial Hospital in Pyongyang in February 1897; and she published a biography of her late husband in August 1897. It was during this time that Rosetta visited the New York Institute for the Blind and drew from New York Point to begin development of Korean Braille.[1]

She returned to Korea in 1897 with her two children to serve in Pyongyang, where she had begun pioneering mission work with her husband and had endured severe persecution. Shortly after her arrival, however, her 3-year-old daughter, Edith Margaret, died of dysentery. Rosetta suffered greatly from this loss, even more so than when she had lost her husband. She wrote in her diary a letter to her dead daughter:

> "Mamma can't help longing for a happier experience, and she has tried to lay her Isaac on the altar, and to let God do with her the best he can; and even where she may not have succeeded in this, it seems as if God himself has taken her most precious things, and she has tried to learn the lessons He would have her, and not be rebellious."

---

[1] The first embossed book for the blind of Korea, the syllabary and first six lessons from Mrs. George Heber Jones' 초학언문 *Chyo Hók Eun-Mun* (*A Korean Primer* - nine cards, about 5½ x 9 inches, pricked on oiled Korean mulberry paper by hand in 1897), was donated to Taegu University School of Special Education by her granddaughter Phyllis Hall King in 1996 and is currently on display at the Rosetta Hall Museum Room.

Rosetta's faith is remarkable in the face of her great personal losses. Despite her lack of understanding over their meaning, she said she "must just give her feelings over to Jesus and trust him implicitly."

In the summer of 1901, Dr. Rosetta Hall returned to New York for the second time, physically and mentally exhausted. After recuperating at the Castile Sanatorium for eight months, she again returned to Korea in the spring of 1903. Until her retirement in 1933, she remained steadfast in her work. She founded the Women's Medical Training Classes in Pyongyang and Seoul; her class in Seoul would later become the Women's Medical Institute, the precursor to Korea University's College of Medicine. She established four hospitals: the Baldwin Dispensary in Seoul (1892), the Woman's Hospital of Extended Grace in Pyongyang (1894), the Hall Memorial Hospital in Pyongyang (1897), and the Chemulpo Woman's Hospital (1921). She also helped to establish the Edith Margaret Children's Wards in Pyongyang and the Child's Welfare Clinic in Seoul. Her work on behalf of the blind and deaf gained recognition throughout East Asia, leading to the Convention on the Education of the Blind and Deaf of the Far East, first held in Pyongyang in August 1914. Her forty-three years of service in

Korea were a true testament to her resilience, her bravery, and her spirit. But they also testify to her religious conviction and purpose. In spite of the sacrifices she made and the losses she sustained, her obedience was drawn from the wellspring of her love for God and for the Korean people. God's provision, enacted through Dr. Rosetta Hall and many other devoted workers, liberated Korea's underprivileged—the women, the poor, and the handicapped—and privileged them anew as children of the King.

It is a blessing and an amazing grace that the work of transcribing and translating Dr. Rosetta Hall's diaries fell upon me. A faithful life is most precious in His eyes, and such a life is now able to be recorded, recognized, and passed down through the generations. I thank the Hall family for preserving and donating these diaries. The *Journal of Sherwood Hall*, in particular, passed through many hands in order to survive. Prior to his forced evacuation from Korea by the Japanese, Dr. Sherwood Hall had sent the journal to Miss Lund, who boarded the last evacuation boat to North America, the *S.S. Mariposa*. She brought it with her across the Pacific, and upon her arrival in Los Angeles, she sent it through post to Pastor Scott of Liberty, New York, to whom it arrived safely in December 1940. After

Diary of Dr. Rosetta Hall 1890

Dr. Rosetta Hall's death in 1951, two generations of the Hall family—her son Dr. Sherwood Hall, his wife Dr. Marian Hall, their daughter Mrs. Phyllis Hall King, and her husband Dr. Edward King, Jr.—have preserved these diaries over the course of sixty-four years. On January 1, 2015, Dr. and Mrs. King generously decided to offer the documents to the public.

I spent three days and nights with them in their home in McLean, Virginia, brainstorming about how to best benefit the public with the history, stories, and lessons written in the diaries. I was asked to translate the diaries into Korean and publish them in both Korean and English. In April 2015, all six diaries of Dr. Rosetta Hall (four diaries from 1890 – 1894 and two scrapbooks chronicling Sherwood and Edith's childhoods) were donated to the Yanghwajin Foreign Missionary Cemetery in Seoul, where Dr. Rosetta Hall and her five other family members are buried. The first diary of 1890 was published with a Korean translation in September 2015 as a highlight for Yanghwajin's Special Exhibition commemorating Dr. Rosetta Hall's 150th birthday. The rest of the volumes will be published over the next year.

Readers of both English and Korean will benefit from these volumes. Essentially, they were her scrapbooks. Many letters, photographs, newspaper articles, sketches, and notes, as well as locks of hair, clothing, and pressed flowers and leaves, are preserved in the books as primary sources. She had continued to add notes and memo clips to her original material as the years passed by, writing around the edges and filling in the open margins. I have left her materials and texts mostly in their original state, correcting only a few spelling errors and re-arranging some of the entries to reflect their chronology.

Since her girlhood days on a farm in Liberty, New York, Dr. Rosetta Hall loved God and strained to hear His voice. In spite of doubt and tribulation, she followed Him and obeyed His commands. She went to the land where no one else would go, and she fulfilled the good work that no one else would fulfill. She loved the people no one else seemed to love. She grew from the roots of God's Love and was able to stand up again and again throughout all her storms, in order to convey that Love to others. What a great mind, and a beautiful life!

Diary of Dr. Rosetta Hall 1890

I hope for the readers of these diaries to be blessed and inspired by Dr. Rosetta Hall's example.

Sue Kim
Colorado Springs
December 4, 2015

FREDRICKS, 1890.   24   770 BROADWAY, N. Y.

"Miss Rosetta Sherwood, M.D.
New York Deaconess Home
May 27, 1890
As she did Home Missionary Work
in N. Y. City 1889-90"

August 21, 1890

Let this mind be in you, which was also in Christ Jesus. Phil. ii.5

I was up at 5 a.m. and dressed. Miss Lewis[2] of the New York Deaconess Home and I ate a lunch, and then it was time to say "goodbye," that long goodbye, for five years and perhaps longer. Mother and I said it out in the kitchen as we kissed each other with tears in our eyes—and hearts too, I feel. Then came Father, and I couldn't say one word. He hoped I'd be happy in my work and asked me to remember him in my prayers. Dear old Father, I just wanted to hug him and tell him how much I appreciated him, how very good he has been to me all my life, but my heart was too full I could articulate nothing but silently clung to his hand. Oh dear Lord, if it be Thy will may I find Father, Mother, Annie and my brothers and sisters if my life be spared to return to Liberty some day. Somehow it seems to me that I will see them all here again—if I thought I would not, how much harder it would be for me.

We took a nice box of vegetables down to the Home[3] with us. Had a pleasant journey down, Lewis read to us from *In The Far East*[4], a beautiful book Dr. Hall gave me and which she and I have been reading together.

---

[2] Miss Ella A. Lewis arrived in Korea in 1891 as a trained nurse for the Methodist Episcopal Mission North.
[3] New York Deaconess Home and Training School of the Methodist Episcopal Church.
[4] Likely *Views in the Far East* by Isabella L. Bird.

Arrived at Weehawken [5] 11 a.m. and to our surprise found Dr. Hall waiting for us. He ordered a carriage which took us with our baggage to the Home, arriving there just in time for dinner. It seems quite like a home to me there after spending a happy six months of work there last winter.

I went to see Mrs. Skidmore[6] also Dr. Baldwin[7] but neither were home—did a little shopping at Macy's and returned in time for supper.

About 7 p.m., Dr. Hall called with a cousin of his, a Rev. Mr. Drummond, who is shortly to go to China as a missionary under the Presbyterian Board. Mrs. Dickinson came in and we had a pleasant call.

I was pretty tired when I went to bed, and did not sleep very well.

Am so sorry I shall miss seeing Mrs. Jenkens— didn't answer her last letter thinking I'd see her soon. She has gone to Wilkes-Barre[8] upon her vacation and we have received news of a terrible

Miss Ella A. Lewis

---

[5] Weehawken is a township in Hudson County, New Jersey.

[6] Mrs. H. B. Skidmore was the corresponding secretary of the Woman's Foreign Missionary Society.

[7] Rev. Stephen Livingstone Baldwin (1835 – 1902) was a missionary to China until 1870. During the last 14 years of life, he was the recording secretary of the Missionary Society of the Methodist Episcopal Church.

[8] Wilkes-Barre, Pennsylvania.

cyclone they had there the day she was due, and have not yet heard from her. I wanted to see her so much, and now I feel worried about her.

"Mrs. H. L. Jenkens, New York Deaconess Home, May 27, 1890. She introduced Dr. Rosetta Sherwood to Dr. William James Hall in Nov. 1889."

Nearly all the Deaconesses are away now. "Weickey" hugged me and called me her "dear dear dockie" and in her French way declared she loved me more than anyone else.

16

Dear Mrs. Dickinson, the Superintendant, is as lovely as ever, but sadly in need of rest.

Dr. Bryan is here, and I think she is well liked. I am so glad I could get someone to go on with the medical work which I began: and I am sure Dr. Bryan is just the right one—may the dear Father abundantly strengthen her. She is looking well, and [I] think she will enjoy the work.

August 22, 1890

He became obedient unto death, even the death of the cross. Philip. ii.8

> "When I survey the wondrous cross
> On which the Prince of glory died,
> My richest gain I count but loss,
> And pour contempt on all my pride."[9]

I got up and dressed in time for 7 o'clock breakfast. After prayers led by Miss Lewis, I started out for a day full of business. Went to the postmaster general and got Dr. Carpenter's address. Thought I'd get him to vaccinate me. Have been vaccinated 3 times within last 2 years but unsuccessful—vaccinated myself the last time—think perhaps virus was not fresh. Dr. C. was not in—office home this evening.

I then went to the bookrooms and there fortunately met both Mrs. Skidmore and Dr. Baldwin. Think by leaving the city tomorrow morning, I can manage to get to Frank's to stay over Sunday. I had intended to stay here till Monday,

---

[9] Issac Watts.

but didn't know what rail road I was going on. Will go on the West Shore, and they tell me to get off at Canajoharie[10] for Luzerne.[11] I fear it is not very near, but perhaps I can get someone to take me there. After dinner, Dr. Bryan went with me to the bookrooms and we looked around a little and then Dr. Baldwin went with me to get my ticket to Chicago. He is a very good man, but if Mrs. Skidmore knew how he talked to me about marrying etc. , how that very often the Parent Board had a bill presented to them by the W. F. M. S., which they always cheerfully paid (meaning outfit and passage money of a missionary lady who moves before her five years are up) and if she knew all the love stories he told me about missionaries, I think she would be more careful how she sent him with the W. F. M. S. workers to buy tickets see them off, etc.

I called to see Franklin Hallett & Co., 2-4 Stone Street about my freight, but found Mr. Hallett out. Went up to Ehrich's and purchased a few last "little things" and a packing "telescope" to put my cloth suite in for I find it too warm to wear—shall have to wear my sateen.

After supper, went to Dr. Carpenter's but he had no fresh virus so I shall have to put that little operation off till I get to San Francisco. Sorry tad.

Went on to Mrs. Skidmore's. Bless her great big heart. She is like a mother to me. She says she has perfect confidence in me: she told Dr. Baldwin that Dr. Sherwood would

---

[10] Canajoharie is a village in the town of Canajoharie in Montgomery County, New York.
[11] Luzerne, Pennsylvania.

get to Korea if there was any such thing and when she got there they'd know it. She told me to write her just what I thought of everything there and if there was anything she could do to help me, she'd do it. She gave me one of her pictures taken sitting in her own room by her little table covered with missionary reports, letters, etc. I think so much of it. She also gave me *Crumbs from the King's Table* by Margaret Bottome[12], which had been given to her by the author. It is very nice.

It rained very hard and I didn't get away till about 9 p.m. Found Dr. Hall waiting for me at the Home. Dear Doctor, he doesn't like to see me go, but he doesn't try to stop me now, though he says he could give me up for nothing else but the Master's work. It has been so very hard for me to decide whether the Lord would have me do single service as I had thought best, until Dr. Hall has so earnestly tried to make me think differently. His arguments have at times almost converted me to his way of looking at the subject, that if we would go out together we would be such a help to each other and thus do so much more for our Master, also we would not lose the time of acquiring a new language as one or the other must do should we wait five years. It is all very true, and there are many other things in favor, but it seems to me that my strumous[13] trouble is a barrier that neither of

---

[12] Margaret McDonald Bottome (1827 – 1906), an American columnist and religious organizer, founder of the Christian spiritual development and service organization now known as the International Order of the King's Daughters and Sons. She attended school in Brooklyn and in 1850 married the Reverend Frank Bottome.

[13] Archaic word for scrofulous. A scrofula is a disease with glandular swellings, probably a form of tuberculosis.

us can overlook. Whether it will be better or worse in an Eastern country, we cannot tell. Doctors have always promised me as I grew older I could get rid of it and I think five years from now I can better tell whether it would be wise or not for me to marry anyone. I have several other minor reasons beside, and I trust that I am doing now as the dear Lord wishes. Dr. Hall insists upon making an engagement for 5 years, but I insist upon his being perfectly free to renew or not his offer 5 years from now as he may then see fit. He is a dear good man, one of the Lord's very best I am sure, and I love him more and more as I know him better. My not accepting his love and care for me now is not, not an easy thing for me, but I believe it to be for our best good.

> "Leaning on Thee, with childlike faith
> To Thee the future I confide;
> Each step of life's untrodden path
> Thy Love shall guide."[14]

Saturday, August 23, 1890

Whether we live, we live unto the Lord; whether we die, we die unto the Lord. Rom. xiv.8

> "Lord, give me grace that I may be
> Thine with such soul-sincerity
> That wheresoe'er my steps may move
> My first last thought may be Thy Love."[15]

---

[14] Charlotte Elliott.
[15] Rev. John Samuel Bewley Monsell (1811 -1875).

I awoke quite early, took a bath before breakfast. Miss McSwain led prayers this morning. We read Phil. IV. Mrs. Dickinson picked out the 19th verse for me: "My God shall supply all your needs according to His riches in glory by Christ Jesus." Mrs. Dickinson made such a simple, touching little prayer for my safety upon my long journey by land and by sea. They sang "Jesus Lover of My Soul"—the baggage man came before we quite finished and I had to go and see that off; and in a short time, Mrs. Dickenson came in said my escort had come, and so I bade goodbye to the New York Deaconess Home and its dear inmates parting with many kind wishes for each other. Mrs. Dickenson gave me *A Little Leaven, A Missionary Story*, a story written by one of the Chicago Deaconesses. Dr. Hall had several books for me: *The Shepherd Psalm* by Mr. Meyer, *The Open Secret* and *The Christian's Secret of a Happy Life* by Hannah Whithall Smith, and *Abide in Christ, With Christ*[16], *Like Christ, The Spirit of Christ* and *Holy in Christ* by Andrew Murray. I don't know what Father would say I am sure—he worried because I took so many books in the first place, and now I have had nearly a dozen more given me.

Dr. H. and I took the 9th Avenue Elevated [railway] [17]to Franklin station—we went one station beyond, however, before we knew it, but it was just about as near Jay Street. I got my baggage checked, and as we saw nothing of Dr. Baldwin who thought he'd meet me there to see me off, we

---

[16] *With Christ in the School of Prayer.*

[17] Ninth Avenue El was the first elevated railway in New York City. It opened in 1868 as the West Side and Yonkers Patent Railway, a cable-hauled line. It ceased operation in 1940.

crossed the ferry to Weehawken. It takes nearly half an hour from Jay Street, and it was very pleasant out upon deck. Dr. Hall wished me to promise him if there was anything whatever I should need while in Korea to let him know and he'd procure it for me. I told them I didn't see where the sacrifice of being a missionary came in for my mother, Mrs. Skidmore, Dr. Eleanor Newton, and he, all four had told me that I might call upon them for everything I wanted. He suggested that perhaps the sacrifice for me lay in my allowing them to help me this way. I'd not thought of it in that light before: in truth I had mentally said to myself when he was insisting upon letting him know, that I never would. We talked about a number of things and made a few simple plans for the next five years. He saw me comfortably fixed in a West Shore car and we each said "Goodbye, doctor"—and, and he kissed me for the first time, so naturally, and too quickly for me to think whether it was quite proper or not!

As far as Cornwall, we were along the service road that goes to Liberty: and it was not until I saw the N. Y. O & W R.R.[18] at this point separating from the West Shore—passing farther and farther to the left while we kept to the right (may it indeed be right)—that I really began to realize that here my path in life divided and I am taking the one that leads me far away from home and its loved ones, from all

---

[18] New York Ontario and Western Railroad. Ontario & Western built the North River Railroad from Weehawken to Middletown by way of Cornwall, while the West Shore built from Cornwall north. New York-New Jersey Port and Harbor Development Commission, William Russell Willcox. "History of New York's Railroad Development." *Joint Report with Comprehensive Plan and Recommendations.* Vol. 1 Part 4, 1920, p99.

the dear old associations, to strangers in a distant land. But thanks to our Heavenly Father, we are trusting Him to lead us into paths of usefulness—"The love of God is broader than the measure of man's mind, and the heart of the Eternal is most wonderfully kind." I am so glad that, as Professor Drummond says, love is the universal language, and though I am going to a strange people with an unknown tongue yet I love my work and I shall love them I feel sure, and it will not be long before I shall have friends there: then too I don't have to give up the dear home ones—no not by any means, we can hear from each other, every month, and by and by I hope I shall see them all again, and surely if we may not meet again in this life I trust we do so "know God" as to meet in the life eternal.

"And God help and keep us all safe to permit us to see each other again. This is my daily prayer. Mother"

"West Point Military Academy"

The cars go so roughly. I can scarcely write and so shall defer it for the present.

It is a very pretty trip up the West Shore of the Hudson. When opposite the Catskills[19], I saw one mountain away in the distance which looked exactly like Walnut Mountain[20], the mountain house and all, but suppose it could not have been. At Kingston, we stopped for lunch.

**Leaving New York on N.Y.C. & H.R. Railroad,
trip up the West Shore of the Hudson through Catskills.**

At Canajoharie, I got off. Inquired for Luzerne—no one, not even Delivery man ever heard of it—so I concluded I could not be very near Frank's. I went to the Post Office and inquired and they looked it up for me and said Luzerne was

---

[19] The Catskill Mountains or the Catskills are a large area in the southeastern portion of the U.S. state of New York.
[20] Walnut Mountain in Liberty, New York.

North of Saratoga, Warren County, instead of Fulton and I should have gone to Albany or Schenectady and upon the Adirondack Railroad. Went back to the R.R. Station and found I could not possibly get there now today. Then I found it would cost me about $5 to stay over in Canajoharie, so concluded to take the same train that I at first intended leaving New York upon 5 p.m. Monday: it is due here at 11 p.m. I had to take an upper sleeper but slept well—it was airy and better springs I think than the lower. Its swaying motion soothed me and I am sure I got to sleep easier than I would have in a hotel.

When I went to telegraph to Frank that I was going right on to Chicago, the operator told me there had been a smash up on that road today. So I can thank the Dear Lord that I made a mistake.

August 24, 1890

I arose at about 5 a.m. Washed and dressed—changing cars at Buffalo, taking Michigan Central Railroad, reached the station at Niagara Falls at 7:45 a.m. Eastern time and left it at 7:45 a.m. Central time. I was just eating my breakfast when we came in sight of the wonderful falls— the train stopped a few minutes and I got out

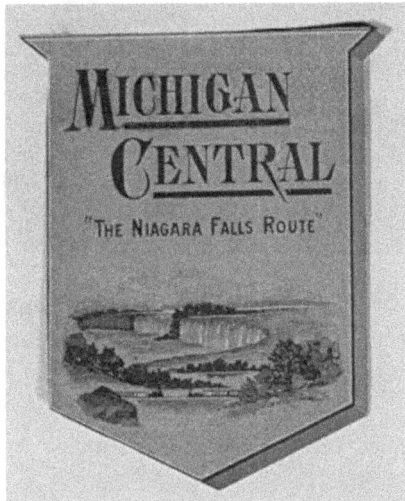

and got a still better view—could see Horse Shoe Falls very well.

Niagara River is pretty—the part I saw had banks of almost perpendicular cliffs covered with green shrubbery. Suspension Bridge I saw in the distance spanning these banks—it looked almost as light and airy as so many spider webs.

We are now in Canada. The land is level. See few stones. Fences are mostly the old fashioned serpentine rail fence. Some board fences, some wire. Noticed quite a number of horses upon the farms. Quite good farm buildings and some stacks of hay.

Bird's-eye View of Niagara River and Falls

Niagara Falls

We are passing along the North side of Lake Erie—
sometimes near enough to the shore to get a delightful view.
Arrived at St. Thomas[21] about 10 a.m. and at Detroit, Michigan at 1 p.m. From here on the cars were so crowded that
nearly everyone had to have a seat mate. I didn't have one
till I reached Jackson[22]. Here, quite a number got on and as
a rather oldish looking gentleman passed through and back
without finding a seat, I moved my valise and asked him to
sit down. He thanked me saying he didn't like to ask a lady
if a seat is occupied, but supposed he might better than to
stand up. I thought he looked like a farmer and as I was writing home, thought it would be a good chance to learn something of Michigan farming. He said wages were high, $20 per
month, and then they didn't do half as much as he used to
for $13. Crops were poor this year because it is so dry. He

---

[21] St. Thomas, Ontario, Canada.
[22] Jackson, MI.

doesn't depend upon raising grain much to sell but raises horses, sold a colt the other day for $1000, one of Loretta F's[23] colts. From farm talk we got upon other subjects. I mentioned I had intended spending some day with my brother who was a minister but missed him by mistake.

He asked if I were a Methodist. I said yes, and asked him how he came to guess it. He said, "Oh, because you are so sober looking." Told him I was sorry that was how he told for I always thought Methodist, were the most happy looking people in the world, and I didn't know before but that I looked happy for I had no reason not to. I asked him if he was a Christian and he said no, then after we talked a little longer he said that he was a "spiritualist," also his wife, daughters and their husbands. He had a grandson who died with Addison's disease. I read him that little tract called a "Child's Question." He said it was very good but it didn't hit him for he had always tried to do as he'd be done by, was charitable and expected to have a home in heaven by and by. I said, "And this is life eternal to know Thee the only true God and Jesus Christ whom thou hast sent"[24] that it didn't make so much difference what we did, at least we could not depend upon that to save us but that we must know God and trust in Jesus for our Salvation. He said yes, he thought he did. I said, "Well, then, you must be a Christian for as I understand it that meant one who believed in Christ and trusted his salvation to His atonement for our sins." He said

---

[23] Loretta F is a Michigan mare that won the Cleveland race in 1887. *National Live Stock Journal*, Volume 18, 1887, p309.
[24] John 17:3.

when I asked him if he was a Christian he thought it meant if he was a Methodist or Presbyterian or something.

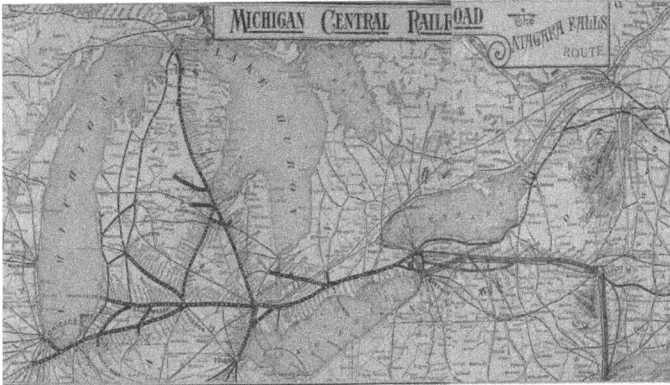

Michigan Central Railroad, Niagara Falls Route

He said he guessed I was out upon some missionary work now, and finally I told him what my mission was, and he became quite interested in it—though he had little faith in missionaries. He asked me many questions about my work. I told him one reason why I had preferred to be a medical missionary was because I preferred to work for Jesus that way—at least it seemed to me it would be more for His glory than to "talk" for as he could see I couldn't do that very well. He said no, he saw I couldn't and beside he thought I was too broad in my views. I told him I thought Christianity was the broadest religion in the world.

Well, we passed the time quite pleasantly all the way to Chicago, and he wished that I'd take a little time when I get to Korea and write how I liked it. I told him I thought I would. He gave me his name, C. C. Pond, Jackson, Michigan. I gave him my card with that tract "The Solitary Way" also "Sometime" with some appropriate Bible verses. Like all other men, he could not under-stand how I could go away there to work without a "companion" as he termed it—he thought it would be so much better and pleasanter. Somehow, I believe men are all agreed upon this one subject if upon no other.

VESTIBULED DINING CARS

The Michigan Central has replaced its old line of Dining Cars with six new ones of the latest designs, containing all the improvements and embellishments that experience could suggest, and they are now without equals in the country. The superior style in which these cars are finished and furnished is only comparable by the excellence of the meals. Quietly and at his ease, the traveler partakes of viands that tempt the epicure, amid tasteful and elegant surroundings, while the charges are so moderate as to excite surprise, and the pleasures of the meal are enhanced by the charming and picturesque panorama that glides past.

I breakfasted in Canada and took my dinner and supper to-gether in Michigan in a vestibuled dining car, $1.

Reached the Deaconess Home in Chicago about 10 p.m. Received a warm welcome from Miss Dryer, the assistant Superintendent and went to bed. Slept very soundly until 6 a.m.

Text for the day was, "He which soweth bountifully shall reap also bountifully." II Cor. ix.6

I found an extra dollar bill in my handbag tonight. Think Mr. C. C. Pond must have dropped it in.

Monday, August 25

In lowliness of mind let each esteem other better than themselves. Philip. ii. 3

Met both Mr. and Mrs. Meyer today. I had met Mrs. Meyer before at New York Deaconess Home. They are a wonderful pair.

I also met Dr. Meta Howard[25] who was my predecessor at the Seoul. She is stopping in Chicago now. I like her very much—she seems like a very good and sensible person. She has told me much that will be of use to me in Korea. She hoped to be sent there again in November and I do hope she may.

Here, I also met Dr. Ida Stevenson[26] who with Dr. Rachel Benn goes to Tientsin, China, where Mrs. Skidmore first wished to send me. She is a nice little lady, and I think it will

---

[25] Dr. Meta Howard (1862-1930) arrived in Korea in October 1887 and was the first female physician for the Methodist Mission. She established a hospital and dispensary, PoKuNyoKwan, in Seoul, served for two years, then returned to the United States in 1889 due to failing health. She did not return to Korea. She was born in Albion, Michigan, graduated from the Women's Medical College of Chicago, died in Kalamazoo, Michigan.

[26] Dr. Ida Stevenson did medical work in Tientsin since 1890 with Dr. Rachel Benn.

be pleasant to journey with her and Miss Bengel[27], who is to come to Chicago tomorrow, across to San Francisco. We are all to go upon the same steamer as far as Japan.

I found, by leaving Chicago at 6 [o'clock] tonight, I can go to Omaha and get into Beatrice[28] 130 miles from there by 4 p.m. tomorrow and then I can meet Dr. Stevenson and Miss Bengel there Thursday 10 a.m. This I did, taking a sleeper from Chicago to Omaha, then a day coach to Beatrice, and a carriage to Cousin Henry Randall's[29] where Uncle Bradley Sherwood[30] lives.

Found them all quite well except Fred the oldest son now at home. They were all so pleased to see me. They have a very pleasant home upon a small farm and have a store in town and some buildings to rent.

Cousins Belle and Carrie are both at home. Belle teaches. Carrie recently graduated from the high school. Both very nice girls.

We had a nice row upon the Blue River[31] at night.

---

[27] Miss Margaret Josephine Bengel was appointed to Seoul in 1890 by Woman's Foreign Missionary Society for educational work. She married Rev. George Heber Jones in 1893 and together they pioneered the work in Chemulpo.

[28] Beatrice, Nebraska.

[29] Henry J. Randall married Polly B. Sherwood, daughter of Bradley Burr Sherwood, in 1862. Frank P. Sherwood, *A Changing America: Seen Through One Sherwood Family Line 1634-2006*, p149.

[30] Uncle Bradley Sherwood was Rosetta's father's younger brother.

[31] Blue River, Nebraska/Kansas.

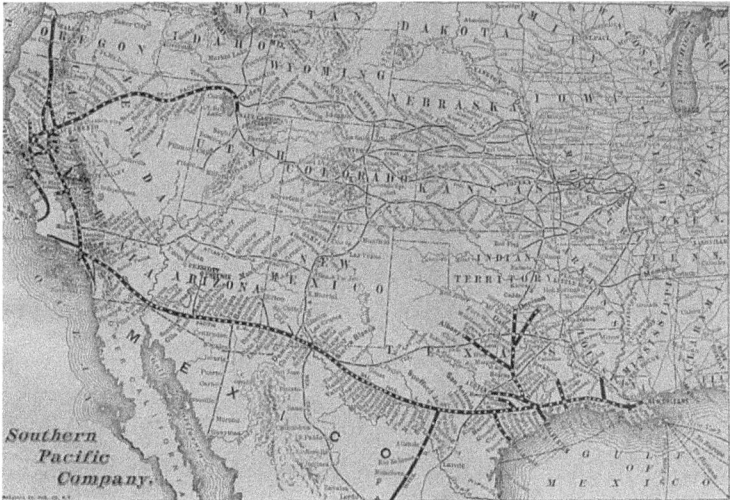

**Chicago to San Francisco on Pacific Railway, through Omaha,
Denver, Cheyenne, Ogden, and Sacramento.**

So far, I've not seen much of the long stretch of prairie, as far as one can see, but except for a ways in Illinois, there have been small hills and streams quite well wooded. Maple, Poplar, Cottonwood and Elm seem the most common. Don't see any evergreens. The farms are quite comfortable look-ing, but most of the houses are small and but one story high. Crossed the Platte [River] coming here—it is pretty low now with islands of land in it at places.

Text today—"Search me, O God, and know my heart: try me and know my thoughts. Ps. cxxxix.23

Wednesday, August 27, 1890

With great mercies will I gather thee. Isa. liv. 7

"Oh, we would bless Thee for Thy ceaseless care
And all Thy works from day to day declare:

Is not our life with hourly mercies crowned?
Does not Thine arm encircle us around?"[32]

The girls drove with me to the city today, and we went all around and saw many pretty places. Went to their brother George[33]'s for dinner. He married a western girl and has a very sensible nice wife I think and two lovely children. Father and mother are both Christians and they have a very happy home.

We intended to drive 7 miles after dinner to see Cousin Stella Reynolds and her daughter Stella whose wedding cards we received just before I left home. I remember Stella when she visited us Centennial year[34]. We corresponded for a time afterward. I did want to see her so much, but it was so intensely hot and as I had to be off upon the 7 p.m. train, we decided it would be too much. So we went back, took supper. I wrote home, bade them all good bye and Belle took me to the depot. I reached Omaha at 12 midnight and stayed in the waiting room till 10 a.m. It was pretty tiresome as it was just a common station with wooden benches and I forgot to take my pillow out of my baggage and it got locked up in the baggage room before I thought.

I wrote a letter of thanks to Mr. C. C. Pond of Jackson, Michigan and enclosed a little tract.

---

[32] Lady Lucy Whitmore.

[33] George Foster Randall carried on 4 generations of family's wall paper, painting & decorating business and operated George F. Randall & Co. He was awarded treasury department medal for civilian activities in raising World War funds. *Who's Who in Nebraska.*

[34] Likely the Centennial Anniversary of American Indepence in 1886.

Had also an interesting talk with the night policeman at the depot upon prohibition[35]. He believes in it as a principle, but does not like the way it works out. He showed me several boxes of liquor bottles directed to a village in Iowa, which had been there, emptied and were on their way back. He has a wife and a pleasant home—he drinks a little occasionally upon cold mornings when upon night duty—is sure he would never be a drunkard—says he'd give it up forever if he thought his wife would want him to, but was quite sure she was not afraid of him. I said she would very likely not own to herself let alone to him any lack of confidence in his strength of character, but nevertheless if he were someone else's husband and she could look at him from the standpoint of a stranger or a friend only, she could not help but to be a little alarmed, as so many policemen form drinking habits and she certainly would feel very happy if she knew he never touched it. He said he didn't know but that was so. I then talked about his influence, that he should not drink liquor for fear it might help to induce others who had not his strength of resistance to habits, etc. From that, we got to speaking of some of Paul's and Christ's sayings—and I found he did not believe in the divinity of Christ. I did so desire to say something to be of real help to him and breathed

---

[35] In the 1820s and '30s, a wave of religious revivalism swept the United States, leading to increased calls for temperance. The state of Maine passed the first state prohibition law in 1846, and the new wave on prohibition at national level was launched in 1906. In January 1920, the 18th Amendment went into effect, by which time 33 states had already enacted their own prohibition legislation. However, in 1932, the Prohibition was eventually ended by the Democratic Party. Though a few states continued to prohibit alcohol after Prohibition's end, all had abandoned the ban by 1966.

a little prayer upward. His time on duty was up soon afterward and he left quite abruptly. I gave him "Communion" and "Sometime" to read and so our paths separated.

August 28, 1890

Without faith it is impossible to please God. Heb. xi.6

I got on the train at Omaha. Dr. Stevenson and Miss Bengel expected me at Council Bluffs[36] as I did not find till after I started that Omaha would be better. Dr. Stevenson expected a friend to meet her in Chicago and go as far as Denver with her. I didn't know whether they had engaged a berth for me or not so went into the day coach until I could see them. I asked the Conductor if there was a party of 3 young ladies in the Pullman[37] car who came from Chicago upon the 6 p.m. train. He asked me their names and I mentioned Dr. Stevenson. At this, a pleasant good looking young lady near me arose and said she was Dr. Stevenson's friend and had missed her Sunday and did not now expect to find her as she supposed her to be upon another railroad. I told her I felt quite sure she would be on this train and as soon as the tickets were taken and the Pullman car unlocked we would see and sure enough we found her all right and the two friends were perfectly delighted for they feared they

---

[36] Council Bluffs, Iowa.

[37] Pullman was used to refer to railroad sleeping cars which were built and operated on most U.S. railroads by the Pullman Company (founded by George Pullman) from 1867 to December 31, 1968.

were not going to see each other again. My stopping off at Omaha seemed to work for good for others beside myself.

Well, I introduced myself to Miss Bengel of Pomeroy, Ohio who goes as a teacher to Seoul. She is only 21 of German descent and reminds me of in appearance very much of Lillian Van Cleef,[38] my friend at the O. N. T. S.[39] I think I shall like her.

It took us a long time to pass through Nebraska. We began at last to see the unbroken Prairie so far as the eye could reach without a tree. And we saw the sunset. Crossed the Platte [River]. Boy with popcorn for a nickel. Slept well.

Friday, August 29, 1890

Be kindly affectioned one to another. Rom. xii.10

Reached Denver, Colorado at 9:35 a.m. Saw some of the Rockies with snow. Changed cars here for Cheyenne[40]. I picked a few Colorado wildflowers to press. We rode in the day coach to Cheyenne—saving 75 cents apiece then there enjoyed two berths for the night. The Pullman was quite well filled then, but after that a party of 8 ladies, teachers in Salt Lake City, came on so we were quite crowded.

---

[38] Mrs. Lillian Van Cleef Whitman (1865-1895) was a Baptist missionary to China, died in Swatow, China. http://www.rootsweb.ancestry.com/~nyseneca/restvale.htm
[39] Oswego Normal and Training School. *History of the First Half Century of Oswego State Normal and Training School 1861-1911*. The Radcliff Press, Oswego, N.Y., 1913, p333.
[40] Cheyenne, WY.

Street view, Denver, Colorado

We noticed two Gentleman and their wives who we think are medical at least and we rather think they belong to our missionary party, but we have not had occasion to speak to them yet.

At Great Canyon Wyoming got a couple of specimens of stone.

We are getting among the most wonderful mountains. The grade up is so gradual that we scarcely realize it but before we know it we are upon top of Mount Sherman, Wyoming, 8247 feet above the sea—the highest point of this railroad. A large pyramid here is in honor of Oaks Ames[41] who was the moving spirit in putting the minor Pacific Railroad

---

[41] Oakes Ames (1804 – 1873) was an American manufacturer, capitalist, and member of the United States House of Representatives from Massachusetts. As a congressman, he is credited by many historians as being the single most important influence in the building of the Union Pacific portion of the transcontinental railroad.

through. Here some of the passengers complained much of not being able to breathe and some of deafness with queer feeling in the head, some had nosebleed, all due to the rarity of the air—so much less dense. All that I personally noticed was a desire for the windows to be open thinking then I could get a little more to breathe—my respiration was 20 per minute, so also was Miss Bengel's—our pulses didn't seem affected.

After passing Mount Sherman, we went over a deep gorge upon the rim bridge.

See low log and mud houses here and there. Noticed one white schoolhouse.

August 30, 1890

Passed through the most of the southern part of Wyoming at night. In the morning after passing Evanston, Wyoming (saw Bear River near Evanston) from there on to Ogden, Utah—the mountain scenery grows still more wonderful. Such steep bare mountains, red stone cliffs scarcely any shrubbery and no trees. One place called the Devil's Slide, 200 feet high, 10 feet wide, a long stretch of smooth rock with raised ridges upon either side—a little beyond is the Devil's gate, a sudden break among the cliffs with a small waterfall—and farther is a tall rock "The Pulpit," this is in Utah and is where Brigham Young stood, preached his first sermon and took possession of the land.

Reached Ogden about 12 o'clock. Crossed Ogden River several times. Here we change cars again for the last time.

Engaged a section and a lower berth through to San Francisco. By some mistake they engaged us Section No. 10, which we found occupied by parties who said they had telegraphed ahead for it. It was settled by allowing us the vestibule for the same money so we can go in style and comfort the rest of the way.

One of the young doctors and his wife are right near us and today we became acquainted—they are Dr. and Mrs. McCartney[42] of Ohio who go to China in our party. (And the other couple was Dr. Jones[43] and Mrs. Dr. Jones[44] who I heard of in New York about the time I left. Dr. Hall told me of them visiting the medical missions. They have gone to Salt Lake City and we will meet them later in San Francisco.) Have had several pleasant little chats with Dr. McCartney and wife. They are both young, not more than 24 or 25 if that? He just graduated and had one year work in hospital. They are both nice looking and are very agreeable people. Seem earnest in our Master's work.

We changed time again now one hour earlier again when we leave Ogden.

Soon we came to the northeast part of Salt Lake. My, what a lake! It stretches far far away—and all so bevel and white about it. The heat here is scorching. It is about 12

---

[42] Dr. and Mrs. J. H. McCartney were appointed by Methodist Episcopal Church to do medical mission work in China.

[43] Dr. Thomas R. Jones was assigned by Methodist Episcopal Church to do medical work in China.

[44] Mrs. Stella B. Jones, M.D., a graduate of Medical College of Chicago, was appointed to China with her husband Dr. Thomas R. Jones.

o'clock western time and about two hours from now we come in sight of the northeast part of this big lake—and again we see it for quite a long time. This part is even prettier—it looks cooler and the blue mountains beyond form a pleasant background. 126 miles by 45.[45]

Just before this we took dinner at Promontory above 5000 feet, 53 miles from Ogden, 780 [miles] from San Francisco. Here May 10, 1869 occurred the most important railroad wedding of the world when men from many states and nations met to celebrate the union of the East and the West by an unbroken track of railroad.[46]

Soon after, we pass to the north of the Great American Desert. Oh what a stretch of bare white sand under the blazing sun. I am so glad that we have not to cross it.

The sandy plains here are covered with a little growth of mountain sage, black sagebrush, and greasewood. The cattle browse upon the sage and grow fat upon it.

Before reaching Ogden, noticed some little farms down in between the mountains where they had good potatoe crops, also vegetables and wheat and some were busy cutting grass and making hay.

But beyond the Promontory there are a few cattle ranches and that is about all.

---

[45] Rosetta probably meant 126 x 45 kilometers. The Great Salt Lake is 120 km (75 miles) long, 45 km (28 miles) wide at present time.
[46] On May 10, 1869, a golden spike was driven at Promontory, Utah, signaling the completion of the first transcontinental railroad in the United States.

We had a shower which has made the air delightfully cool now—and we saw a most beautiful rainbow.

Just now there is a pretty golden sunset over beyond the hill at my right.

This air is a luxury to breathe. We have been passing between the Black Hills and the Rockies and are now in Nevada. Miss Bengel just came in and gave me a small stone which she secured for me at our last stop.

I must go now and get my lunch. 6 o'clock. Suppose it is 9 o'clock home and the folks are just going to bed.

We breakfasted in Wyoming, took dinner in Utah, and supper in Nevada.

I had a lower berth tonight and slept well till 3 a.m. I woke and took a sponge bath from head to foot. It is so crowded in the morning when everyone wants to go to dressing room at once that I thought I'd take my chance now. Went back to bed and slept well till 6 a.m.

Text for the day—"The eternal God is thy refuge and underneath are the everlasting arms."[47]

Sunday, August 31, 1890

Every word of God is pure. Prov. xxx.5

"Lord, Thou art true, and oh, the joy,
            To turn from other words to Thine,
    To dig the gold without alloy
            From Truth's unfathomable mine!"

---

[47] Deuteronomy 33:27.

A gentleman upon the train has just been showing us some specimens containing gold ore. They were quite pretty and the gold was sparkling and bright in some.

We are passing through Reno Valley, which seems to be very fertile. They raise "Lucerne"[48] or Chili clover mostly, can cut 4 or 5 crops in a season. It is sowed from seed first obtained in South America. It looks something like our red clover. This is western Nevada. Crossing Truckee River.

We see mountains with snow upon them now and then. Granite Range[49].

Have seen several groups of Indians this morning. Got off one place and saw a woman with her papoose[50] fastened to a board with sort of a cradle formed over the head with a red handkerchief over it. We raised that up and saw the little dark face with eyes closed fast asleep. One of the gentlemen gave the mother a "nickle" and that made her smile.

The mountains we are passing through now are pretty well covered with evergreen trees. They look like a pine mostly.

Miss Bengel took out of her baggage this morning a letter that Dr. Howard wrote me after I left there, also a package that Mrs. Dickinson forwarded from the Home.[51] It was from Dr. Newton and I have just opened it—a pretty little

---

[48] Alfalfa
[49] Granite Range is a mountain range in Nevada west of the town of Gerlach and the lower Black Rock Desert playa.
[50] A Native American child.
[51] New York Deaconess Home.

flask of smelling salts and a very nice soapbox with Cashmere Bouquet soap. It seemed so nice to get a letter and a present away out here in Nevada from my old friends.

I think we must be finding our way through the Sierra Nevada Mountains now.

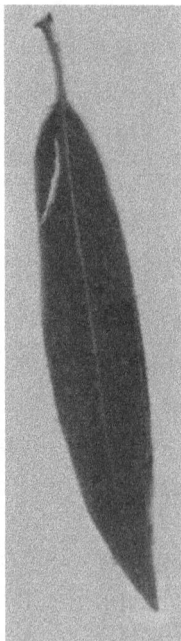

We are following along the course of the Truckee River toward its source. The grade is so heavy we only go at the rate of 8 miles an hour.

We passed some large ice houses filled from ponds drawn from the Truckee. I have been standing out upon the rear platform with Dr. and Mrs. McCartney and another gentleman and wife. At one stop, the doctor got off and got us all a drink from a beautiful mountain stream. He nearly got left. There are a few quite nice looking homes here and there. Saw three little girls in white who seemed to be going to Sunday school. It is 10 a.m.

A leaf from the Sierra Nevada Summit

The mountains are very steep and look well wooded. The banks of the Truckee are all covered with driftwood.

There are quite a number of snow sheds built along this road—noticed one dug through rock. There are lumber shoots upon the mountains. By and by we will see how they wash mountains down for gold I suppose, as we have just crossed the line into California.

At the town of Truckee, we passed the largest lumber yard I've seen in the West.

We also passed the Eastern bound Mail train and sent the letter I've been writing to Dr. Newton.

We are going up over the Sierra Nevada Mountains now in a zigzag through snow sheds almost constantly as we rise higher and higher; we look down and see the snow sheds we have passed through. Can see snow now upon mountains quite near us. We will soon be at the Summit over 7000 feet.

They don't light up much and passing through these sheds is like one long tunnel. We caught a few pretty views of Lake Donner through the openings in the shed, and later got a fine view. It is a very large mountain lake. A gentleman near told me it was named for a family who tried to cross it in the winter and were all frozen to death. I asked him how people knew of it. He said they found the bodies next spring. Then I said how did they know their name was "Donner." He said that was too much for him. I told him Mother always said I asked too many questions.

Now we are at Summit, the highest part of the Sierra Nevada that we passed over 7000 feet. I picked me a little branch of willow, a leaf of which I will put in here.

There is a high hotel built here but the people around seem very rough. I think they need a little home missionary work. By the way, I had Miss Lewis' picture in my book which she gave me just as I came away, and I showed it to a little girl that came to sit by me a few minutes, and then several other people near asked to see it, and then became quite interested in what I told them of New York Deaconess work.

1:35 p.m. Stopped here for lunch and before the train went on, they discovered that a wheel under our coach was cracked—so they had to stop long enough to put on another. It was about 3:15 o'clock before we got started again. We will either be late in San Francisco or else have to move very fast.

Gems of Sierra—Donner and Cascade Lakes

SCATTERED here and there throughout the valleys and gorges of the Sierra Nevada Mountains, from Shasta to Tehachapi, are a thousand lakes, which are to the mountain tops like emeralds in a crown, and are considered by many as the most exquisite gems in the California diadem. Some of these beautiful bodies of water are without rivals anywhere, conspicuously Lakes

GEMS OF THE SIERRA—DONNER AND CASCADE LAKES.

Tahoe, Donner, Webber, Independence, Cascade, Echo, Fallen Leaf, and others. Donner lake is immediately upon the line of the railroad, and perpetuates the name of the head of a party of eighty-one men and women who were overtaken by tremendous snows near its margin in the winter of 1846, of whom more than one-third perished from starvation and cold. This lake is three miles long and half that distance wide at its greatest width, and is reached by the cars of the Southern Pacific Company.

We have been passing through snow sheds now for 40 or 50 miles. It is rather tiresome. Can't see anything and it is too dark to read or write with any comfort.

We now begin to see some fruit orchards loaded with the much talked of California fruit. Saw some [vineyards.]

Placer Co. Cal.

The largest cherry tree in California

Now every once in a while we see large places in the mountains washed out for gold. Sometimes whole mountains are washed down in the valley.

The most wonderful ravines are upon my left as I write—too grand to describe. If the word "immense" had not been so misused by some, I think it would answer very well to describe these ravines in one word.

Tokay vineyard and grapes at Loomis, Placer County, California

At Newcastle, saw the first church I've seen in a long time. There are nice fruit farms from now in good farm-houses, roads, etc., but just now it is very dry. Here is where Aunt Kate and family live.

View from the Coast Range to the Sierra

Soon after leaving Sacramento, "we three" had supper— our last meal on board of train. It was very nice. After this, a gentleman came to my side and asked if my name was "Sherwood".

I looked up and found it was Cousin Charley Bonney[52]. Uncle Robert[53] gave him the telegram I sent from Ogden and he came over to meet me.

It made it very nice for us all to have someone who understood when and where and how to go.

We crossed Sacramento River upon the cars. The whole train being run after a Ferry-boat and so ferried across.

Pear Tree thirty-five years old, bearing 600 lbs. annually.

35-year-old pear tree, bearing 600 pounds annually

---

52 Charles O. Bonney was Rosetta's mother's sister Elizabeth Gildersleeve Bonney's son.
53 Uncle Robert was Rosetta's mother's brother.

General view of Pleasants Valley and the northern part of Sacramento Valley: top left—Starting point of the early vegetable business; top right—Salway peaches; bottom—Snow-capped Mount Shasta visible 200 miles away, and Marysville Buttes 60 miles

At Oakland, we left the train. Cousin Chas took Miss Bengel and my big telescope bags and carried them for us, and we were soon upon the steamer making our way to San Francisco. Arrived at the Occidental Hotel, where we missionaries have special rates made for us, at 11 p.m., but they were full tonight. So we went to the Palace Hotel till the next day. The Palace Hotel is said to be the biggest in the world (?) I believe and it is a very fine one. Dr. Stevenson and I have a large well furnished room with double bed and bath-room. Paid $2 apiece. I had a nice bath and got to bed about 12 midnight. I have been troubled ever since last night with urticaria, probably due to so many changes in water.[54] I slept pretty well.

Scene in Fruit Vale, Oakland, California

September 1, 1890

Dr. McCartney and wife and Dr. Stevenson and I break-fasted together at 9 a.m. (Miss Bengel was met by a friend at the depot and didn't go to the hotel with us.) They brought such an abundance of everything we ordered that if we had only ordered for one it would have been enough for all four.

---

[54] Rosetta added later, "Found later it was due to fleas!"

They brought nearly the whole of a medium sized watermelon for instance to each one.

Cousin Chas met us soon after and piloted us down to the Occidental where we were given rooms 235 and 236, rather small rooms upon the fourth floor.

Poor little Mrs. McCartney was home sick and cried this morning.

After making arrangements at the hotel, Miss Bengel and a friend met us and Cousin Chas piloted us down to the *Oceanic*, the vessel we are to sail in Thursday.

After making arrangements at the hotel, Miss Bengel and a friend met us and Cousin Chas piloted us down to the *Oceanic*, the vessel we are to sail in Thursday.

We made a tour of it, and think she is quite fine, and that we may be comfortable there for three or four weeks. We then went to exchange our orders for tickets. This took nearly 3 hours! We are all mixed up. Dr. McCartney and wife have state-room No. 3, Dr. Stevenson No. 5, Miss Bengel No. 25, and I No. 27. They would allow us to change so that we three girls could be together.

We got back to the hotel after the dinner hour, so Cousin Charley took Dr. S. and myself to a French restaurant for dinner. Then he and I went to see Cousin Sherman Darbee[55]. He keeps a restaurant for men, and seems to be doing a good business. He looks real well. Had a nice call and went back to hotel. Uncle Robert called to see me when I was at dinner tonight but they told him I was out, so he went away again.

SAN FRANCISCO —{ California }—

---

[55] Sherman Darbee is Rosetta's mother's sister Harriet Gildersleeve Darbee's son.

Text today—"The earth shall be full of the knowledge of the LORD, as the waters cover the sea." Isa. xi.9 What a wonderful promise!

Tuesday, September 2, 1890

The Lord is a God of knowledge, and by him actions are weighed. I Sam. ii.3

"He who best does his lowly duty here,
Shall mount the highest in a nobler sphere:
At God's own feet our spirits seek their rest,
And he is nearest Him who serves Him best."[56]

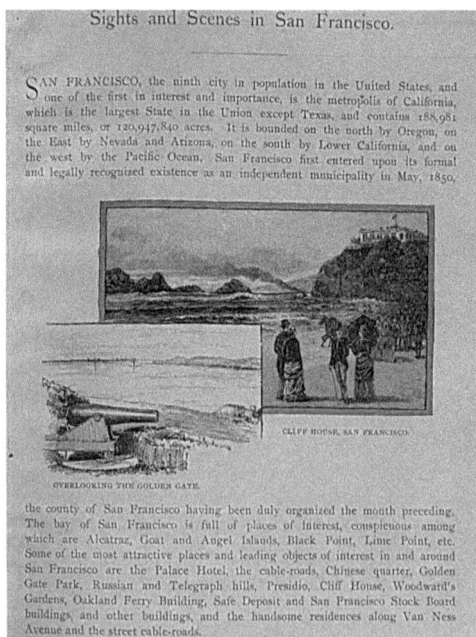

Sights and Scenes in San Francisco

---

[56] Samuel Greg (1804-1877). From hymnal "Stay, Master, Stay."

We arose quite early, breakfasted, and started with Cousin Charley for Sutter[57] Heights and the Cliff House. He brought me a letter from mother, also from Dr. Hall—dear loving letters both of them. I can't help but to think now and then how much easier and more pleasant it would have been had I done as Dr. H wished, waited another year and went out with him: but above everything else I desire to do my duty, however "lowly" or unpleasant it may be for me now, and I think I am where the Lord would have me to be, and by and by we will see "why." It may not be my way, it may not be thy way, but it will be His own blessed way—and Dr. Hall and I both feel willing to trust it all to Him who doeth all things well.

Stutter Heights and Park is, I believe, the finest place I ever was in. Flowers and foliage in luxurious abundance, statues here and there, and everything arranged so nicely and kept in such perfect order—a beautiful green house. At the Cliff House, we could look out toward the Golden Gate, through which we are soon to sail. Just off the shore from the cliff are a couple of islands upon which there are a lot of seals, taking their comfort, some very large ones. Sea gulls flying around.

After spending a very pleasant time, we returned to the hotel for dinner 2 p.m., after which we went out shopping. Bought our steamer chairs and a few little last articles.

---

[57] Rosetta probably meant Sutro Heights. Adolph Sutro acquired the cottage and an adjoining land in 1881 and renovated it into his Sutro Heights Home. He also purchased the adjacent 21.21 acres as well as 80 acres of shore lands, which included Cliff House, the restaurant.

The Chinese quarter of San Francisco

This evening at 7:30, we attended a reception given in the honor of our missionary party (some 14 I believe), by Bishop Fowler[58] in his beautiful San Francisco home. The

---

[58] Bishop Charles Henry Fowler (1837-1908), who was elected Missionary Secretary of the Methodist Episcopal Church in 1880 and Bishop in 1884, has played an important role in Korea Mission. On

house was filled. We left quite early. Met tonight Dr. Jones and Dr. Jones, Rev. Taft and wife who are at the hotel with us.

Wednesday, September 3, 1890

How much more shall your heavenly Father give the Holy Spirit to them that ask him? Luke xi.13

We all went to the Mint[59] this morning. It is the largest in the world—saw them making lots of money, and saw vaults containing millions of dollars.

Went back to the hotel and met the Rev. Mr. Masters by appointment. He took us to an exchange bank and we got our money changed into gold, and into drafts upon Yoko-hama.

February 23, 1885, he wrote from San Francisco to Dr. R. S. Maclay, the superintendent in Japan, saying: "We desire you to act as superinten-dent of Korea, and Brother Appenzeller as assistant superintendent under your direction. Dr. Scranton will act as treasurer of Korea Mis-sion." Bishop Fowler already had ordained Dr. William B. Scranton to Korea on December 4, 1884 while in New York. On February 2, 1885, he also ordained Rev. Henry G. Appenzeller, who had speedily arrived in San Francisco, to Korea.
John Morrison Reid, *Missions and Missionary Society of the Methodist Episcopal Church, Volume 3*. Eaton & Mains, New York; Curts & Jen-nings, Cincinatti, 1896, p495.
William Elliot Griffis, *A Modern Pioneer in Korea: The Life Story of Henry G. Appenzeller*. Fleming H. Revell Company, 1912, p90.
[59] The United States Mint to produce circulating coinage for the United States.

After dinner, Cousin Chas took Dr. S. and myself to Golden Gate Park—it has a beautiful name and is a lovely park. There is a fine Horticultural Hall, children's playgrounds, herd of deer and elk, band stand, walks and drives, etc.

We also went to see a section of the Big tree which is to be taken to Chicago 1892. It was 300 feet high and 99 feet in circumference. It is 3000 years old. We went inside of it, quite a large room where over 100 school children have been at one time—next Sunday, a marriage ceremony is to take place in it. I got a small sample of the wood. It is a red cedar I believe. We took in the "Diamond Palace" on our way back and this with our many long rides downhill and over hills and through valleys upon the cable cars with the buildings we could see completed the most of what we saw in San Francisco. It is a pretty city—nearly all wooden houses which are for the most part separate houses by themselves, few flats or tenement houses. The most curious parts are the hills and valleys with cars running up hill just as fast as they do down. The grass and foliage here is green the year-round. Seldom have rain except in the rainy season.

Got back to hotel 4 p.m. Did our packing and some writing. Uncle Robert spent the evening with me. I like him ever so much and am sorry I could not have seen more of him. He gave me a lot of New York maple sugar, also a $20 gold piece which he gives to every one of his nieces who comes to see him—I am the third. Cousins Minnie and Elsie Gildersleeve were the others. He also gave me a good picture of him. I gave him mine, and my address in Korea and the little track "Communion" and we kissed each other "goodbye."

I wrote to Miss. Lewis and went to bed 10 p.m.

> The Rev. T. De Witt Talmage says of them: "Who that has seen them can think of them without having his blood tingle? Trees are now standing there that were old when Christ lived. These monarchs of foliage reigned before Cæsar or Alexander; and the next thousand years will not shatter their scepter. They are the masts of the continent, their canvas spread on the winds while the old ship bears on its way through the ages. Their size, of which travelers speak, does not affect me so much as their longevity. Though so old now, the branches of some of them will crackle in the last conflagration of the planet."

**Rev. T. De Witt Talmage's[60] quote about trees
on the Sierra Nevada Mountains**

BIRD'S-EYE VIEW OF SAN FRANCISCO.—FROM A PHOTOGRAPH BY WATKINS.

Bird's-eye view of San Francisco-from a photograph by Watkins

---

[60] Rev. Dr. Thomas De Witt Talmadge (1832-1902) was a minister in the Reformed Church and Presbyterian Church in America. He was one of the most prominet religious leaders in the U.S. during the mid-to late- 19th century.

Thursday, September 4, 1890

Cast thy bread upon the waters: for thou shalt find it after many days. Eccl. xi.1

"No act falls fruitless; none can tell
How vast its power may be,
Nor what results enfolded dwell
Within it silently."

My last morning upon land for some time at least. Had breakfast at 8 a.m. Our baggage got off soon after 9 [o'clock]. I wrote a postal home, and one to Mrs. Jenkens, and began a letter to "my doctor William" but we had to go to the steamer before I finished, so I ended it in my state-room. Cousin Chas will mail it for me.

I went out on deck after, and met the Rev. Dr. Harris whom Dr. Baldwin of New York referred me to with Mr. Masters. Also met some more of our party. Rev. Headland and wife and Rev. Mr. Wheeler[61]—also Choung Sing, an Oakland Sunday school boy who returns to China. A Miss Richardson and Miss Smithey and Rev. Lucas and Dr. Campbell sent out by the Methodist Episcopal South—they have been in the Chicago training school.

Soon after my baggage and myself was comfortably fixed in No. 27, a Russian and his wife came and also presented a ticket for 27, but their number was over 20 lower

---

[61] Rev. L. N. Wheeler, D.D. was a missionary of Methodist Episcopal Church to China.

in the engagements—in fact, they only got into San Francisco today while my lower berth in No. 27 was engaged before I came: so I thought I had the best of them: all the same now they came with two big steamer trunks, and lots of valises, bundles, and boxes. I spoke about it to the Chief Engineer who is a very kind good-natured gentleman and he said the "Purser"[62] would settle it after we started.

I am so glad I had none of the dear home folks to bid goodbye to as the gong sounded for all who did not belong on board to be off. And a little later we let loose from land and sailed away toward the Golden Gate. It was so foggy that we very soon lost sight of land.

I went to the Purser and showed him my ticket. He said evidently the room had been sold twice, and if there was another whole state-room, he could change the Russian and his wife, but there was not, so he wished me to go into No. 19 with a Mrs. Cook. I went there to see how things looked and found two women who claimed to belong there, and later out upon deck found that Miss Smithey also had a ticket calling for No. 19, so I took her and went to the Purser (who by the way is a very kind and considerate gentlemen. I take it) and told him I had decided to go to [No.] 19 but found three there so of course I couldn't as there were only berths for three counting the lounge. So here was another room that was sold twice. Finally, I was settled in No. 5 with

---

[62] The purser in a ship is the officer responsible for all administration and supply; frequently the cooks and stewards answer to him as well.

Mrs. Vogel, Dr. Stevenson going into [No.] 25 with Misses Bengel and Richardson.

We had lots of fun eating lunch about 3 o'clock. We all sat where we were a mind to and my party happened to get together. Dr. Jones and I demolished a lot of sweet potatoes and we all ate a pretty fair meal though several complained of the rolling of the boat and their heads and Mrs. McCartney got sick and had to leave us quite early.

After lunch, we all got out our steamer chairs upon the upper deck and tried to take things easy.

So far I have not felt a bit sick, not much different from going to Staten Island. There is such a heavy fog that we are not going very fast.

After 6 p.m., the dinner gong sounded. Now like school children, we are each assigned to our respective places. When I asked the Steward where "Sherwood" was down for I thought I heard him say something about the Purser as he showed me the way; and sure enough, what was my surprise to be seated by this gentlemen. I wondered if it just happened so (?). I have not learned his name yet, but find he began at one time to study medicine at Bellevue [63], but stopped on account of his eyes which have been treated by Dr. Roosa.[64] He also knows Dr. Emerson.[65] Here is a little coincidence—he told me Dr. Emerson (Dr. Roosa's partner)

---

[63] Bellevue Hospital Medical College in New York.

[64] Daniel Bennet St. John Roosa (1838 - 1908) was a well known ophthalmologist and otologist, the founder and president of the New York Post-Graduate Medical School.

[65] Nathaniel Bright Emerson (1839 –1915) was a medical physician and author of Hawaiian mythology. He was the son of Protestant missionary Rev. John S. Emerson and father of artist Arthur W. Emerson.

was born within 10 miles of him in Virginia. I told him Dr. Roosa's birthplace was within 10 miles of mine in New York. We had both attended clinics at the Manhattan Eye and Ear Hospital. So altogether we had a pleasant meal—though the ship began to rock and pitch pretty well for me.

When I went to my room, it had such a peculiar odor that it made me feel a little sick so I came up into the "Social Hall" and fixed myself very comfortable in one corner and felt perfectly well—it was airy and nice. Dr. Jones came and settled near me and we had a little conversation, what I find is a wonderful help to me when I begin to feel a little sick if I can talk to someone I forget it. After a little I began to feel sleepy, and as Dr. Jones was snoring, I thought perhaps I'd better go to my room and see if my baggage had been changed. I found it had all right. But going through the hall that peculiar sickening odor (learned, for me and least, that sickening odor was the sign of seasickness, which if I wished avoid, must go to my berth and get settled before eating!) struck me again and my room was so closed I began to feel a little uneasy as I unpacked my nightdress, etc. About this time my roommate Mrs. Vogel began to vomit, and soon I followed suit! I brought up about a quart I should think, and thought from the looks of it, "No wonder I vomited. Hope I'll know enough not to eat so much again." I felt relieved afterward, and for a time felt all right, but before I got fixed in bed, I threw up once more. I have not vomited before since I can remember. It is not nearly as hard for me as I was afraid it would be, and I do not feel so deathly sick as some complain of. My head keeps all right. I have been taking some Sodium Bromide as a preventative, but tonight I threw it up, and it seems as if I could not take it again.

I was comfortable the rest of the night and slept fairly well, though my couch was pretty hard.

**List of passengers per S.S. Oceanic,
sailing from San Francisco September 4, 1890**

Friday, September 5

O magnify the LORD with me, and let us exalt his name together. Psa. xxxiv.3

"The free-will offering of our lives
To Thee O Lord, we raise."

I felt just as well as ever when I got up this morning at 6 a.m. and for some time after. Before I got quite dressed I thought perhaps it would be better if I ate something, so I ate the juice of a whole bunch of grapes. All went lovely for a while, but I had to be in the little closed room so long unpacking so as to get at some heavy wraps for the deck, and the ship did roll so that it was not long before I was crying "Europe" again. As soon as I could I got from my room and went to the kitchen and asked the Chinese cook there for some chipped beef which he gave me. I then went up where I was last night, lay down on the lounge, and chewed beef. Soon felt much better. The breakfast gong sounded and I went down. The Purser said he did not expect to see me this a.m. I ate some dry toast and a little coffee, and it went very well. But when I went to my room to fix for the deck, I felt sick again. I chewed beef and it passed off. I have my cloth dress and jacket on and my deaconess cloak, and my checked shawl, and yet I am not warm enough in my steamer chair on deck. I stayed there till noon however for I felt so much better than indoors. Once the vessel went over such a great swell that when we came down the deck was so steep that many of the people in chairs just slid and tumbled right along to the outside railing! It made quite a scramble. Sometimes when we would go down on the other side of a mountain swell, my breakfast felt as if it would like to go with it, but by dint of chewing the smoked beef, I managed to keep it down and to do some reading and writing. By lunch time again, I felt pretty good. We are now nearly 300 miles from land and it is a beautiful sunshiny day. Now I see the Ocean does look a beautiful blue what little I ever saw of it before looked more of a green, but today it is an Indigo blue with here and there great caps of white, as far as the eye can see nothing else unless once in a while a sea gull.

At lunch, I ate dry toast, rare beef, and a little weak coffee, and it tasted pretty good, and has not wanted to come up yet, though I was in my room quite a little while too. A few more ladies down to lunch. Drs. McCartney, Jones and wives not around yet, neither is the Rev. Headland. His wife was to breakfast but not to lunch. Drs. Joneses just got around this evening but did not come to dinner—think the married people don't get along as well as the single. Mr. and Mrs. Brown[66] of the M.E.C. South are both in their berths yet also.

---

[66] Rosetta added later, "More than 22 years later[1912], Rev. Dr. O. E. Brown (and Mrs. Brown), Professor of Church History at Vanderbilt University and representing the Education Committee of Edinburgh Conference Continuation Committee stopped with me in Pyong Yang over Sunday. I remembered them, but they didn't seem to have remembered Miss Bengel or I for Korea, or Dr. Benn or Stevenson for China, though Mrs. Brown was supposed to chaperone both Miss Smithey and Miss Richardson whom we saw so much of. Mr. and Mrs. Brown were newly married and I remember they seemed very exclusive and paid little attention to the rest of us. It seems they remained

Miss Bengel and I tried our "sea legs"[67] this afternoon by walking 20 or 30 minutes upon the sunny side of deck. It was lovely, though we did not walk a line by any means. Miss Bengel introduced me to Rev. Mr. Lucas of the Methodist Episcopal Church South who goes out as a missionary to China. He is quite a young man, but fine looking, and I like his ways very much. He came in the Social Parlor and talked to us this evening also. He can't sing, and said he "would have to get someone to sing for him over in China." As I can't sing either I think he must be looking after Miss Bengel a little perhaps.

I enjoyed dinner tonight very much. Had rare roast beef and potatoe, boiled chicken with gravy and bread, tapioca pudding with peaches and nuts. The Purser (I've not learned his name yet) introduced me to Mr. Livingstone of

---

but 2 years in the field. I saw Mr. Brown next at Edinburgh but didn't see him to speak to. They were called home because Vanderbilt needed Mr. Brown. He has been Professor of Church History there now for 20 years, and this is his first time off from that work."
One of the most notable results of the 1910 World Missionary Conference at Edinburgh was its appointment of a Continuation Committee to oversee the work begun by the Conference in the following years. The Continuation Committee appointed nine special committees on particular subjects, of which Committee on Christian Education was divided into two sections – a European section with India and Africa as its field and an American section with the Levant and the Far East as its field. Over the years, there was a significant concentration of efforts on China, East Asia and India, primarily on Christian education and literature. *New-York Observer*, Volume 89, Nov. 17, 1910, p638. *World Missionary Conference Records*, Edinburgh, 1910.
[67] Sea legs is the ability to walk steadily on the deck of a boat or ship. The phrase is used as a metaphor for adjusting to living/travelling at sea.

Pennsylvania, who sits opposite me and they with an occasional word from me now and then carried on quite a lively conversation, the chief topics being mother-in-laws, boyish loves, love and marriage, women's rights, etc. They are both quite interesting gentlemen and appear candid and honest in their manners but I have my suspicions of the Purser that he is a little bit upon the order known as a "ladies man." However, there is more interesting simplicity about him than some I should judge.

This evening, I found Miss Bengel with a bad headache and some other aches. As she is a homeopath and doesn't like to take my drugs, I prescribed a little music for her so we went down in the Saloon and she played upon the piano. Miss Smithey joined us and they two sang. Mr. Lucas came down soon also and by and by Dr. Stevenson and Mr. Wycliff joined us. We spent the time very pleasantly till 10 p.m.

My dinner didn't trouble me at all and I had a good night of it, only waking up once. Think tomorrow night I shall have the upper berth made up instead of the couch as it has springs and will be more comfortable now if I am not sea-sick anymore.

Saturday, September 6, 1890

Blessed is the man whose strength is in Thee. Psa. lxxxiv.5

I feel perfectly well this morning except for that urticaria which the most of our party has been troubled with ever since leaving Chicago or Ogden. I took a compound cathartic pill last night and I am going to take some fruit saline and alkaline bath today.[68]

I enjoyed my breakfast—melon, broiled beef, rice rolls, hash, and finished up with hot rice cakes and maple syrup.

Miss Richardson, the lady Dr. L. R. Meyer sent a note to by me, got down to breakfast for the first this morning. She was put next to me.

I must go now and take my bath. Had a good time and felt better through the day, but at night, the urticaria troubled me again.[69]

At lunch today, nearly everyone was present. We are getting out now where the sea is much quieter. The vessel doesn't rock nearly so much—can walk without much trouble upon deck or anywhere.

How beautiful the water is today. It now looks a purple blue. The weather is fine and we are now getting far enough south so that it is not so cold.

After dinner tonight, Miss Bengel and I took a walk. Mr. Lucas asked permission to join us. Later Miss Bengel joined Dr. Stevenson, and then Miss Smithey joined us. Soon after I excused myself and went into the Social Parlor and read *In The Far East*. About 9 p.m., about the same party who went down last evening went again to the Saloon and we had

---

[68] Rosetta added later, "Still fleas."
[69] Rosetta added later, "Fleas."

some music. At 10 p.m., we broke up. I went to get some books and wraps I left upstairs and when I came down found Miss Smithey, the Purser, and Rev. Lucas still talking in the saloon: they invited me to join them and I did; but I am sorry now I did, or rather that I did not enter my protest to the talk carried on mostly by Miss Smithey[70] between her and the Purser—it was a shame to anyone who believes in Christianity. How any missionary society ever sent her out I don't see—shallow, very superficial—can't even see when she is being made game of—and she makes such absurd remarks—but then I suppose it takes all sorts of people to make a world, and perhaps the dear Lord knows how to make use of her if I don't.

I slept in the upper berth tonight. Slept pretty well, but for the urticaria. Got up 7 a.m. and took a creolin sponge bath. Also vaccinated myself. But tho' I might have gotten rid of one set of fleas, there were always "more to follow."

Sunday, September 7, 1890

Ye are a chosen generation, a royal priesthood, a holy nation, a peculiar people; that ye should shew forth the praises of Him who hath called you out of darkness into his marvelous light. I Pet. ii.9

---

[70] Rosetta added later, "1908—Either I was much mistaken in my idea of Miss Smithey, or getting married and 18 years in the Orient has much improved her, for I find her very companionable as I know her better. Expect I didn't take her right in those days and misunderstanding. Also see September 9th latter part."

"Help us to build each other up,
Help us ourselves to prove;
Increase our faith, confirm our hope
And perfect us in love."

I had quite an interesting conversation with Mr. Livingstone out upon deck this morning—main topic home mission work, little side issues upon woman's great power over man. Mr. L. seems to consider it almost or quite unlimited. I didn't agree. He says men long for petting, coaxing, caressing, etc., much more than is commonly thought. I said I thought we were told these characteristics belonged to woman almost entirely, that man such a strong creature, so absorbed in business etc. that these things had little or no place in his desires. He says that is a mistaken idea.

We had a nice religious service at 10 a.m. conducted by Rev. J. W. Greenwood of the Episcopal Church. Deut. xxxiii was read and some very good chapters from the New Testament. We had nice music and good prayers (read). I enjoyed it all very much. It seems more like Sunday than it did on the cars a week ago today.

Miss Smithey occupied "the Purser" a good part of the morning. At lunch he said to me he had been "longing for this hour" to come. I said, "Have you been working hard?" He said he had been "waiting."

Mr. Lucas and I had a little stroll and then sat down near Rev. Mr. and Mrs. Brown and Miss Richardson soon came along and amused and instructed us by having us guess passages from the Bible the letters of which she indicated by dots. The Rev. Mr. Brown gave one passage, "Little children love one another," but it was decided that it was not in the Bible.

After lunch, our party spent most of the time until dinner by reading aloud in turns *A Little Leaven, A Missionary Story* that Mrs. Dickinson gave me just as I left New York. We all like it a much.

At dinner tonight, Mr. Livingstone and the Purser each drank five glasses of California wine. It is too bad that they cannot see the harm.

After dinner, I was introduced by Dr. Jones to Dr. Campbell, a very young looking young man who belongs to the missionary party of the Methodist Episcopal Church South. Later in the evening, I saw him smoking a pipe—so I don't care to pursue the acquaintance to any great extent.

Rev. Lucas begins to show rather more interest in me than will perhaps prove wise. He is a very fine young man and a real southern gentleman, son of a doctor. I like him very much, and enjoy his company, but when he begins to talk about my teaching him medicine and whether I might accept a medical call from Korea to Shanghai etc., I think I better be wary, considering the source these remarks and similar ones came from—of course from some people they'd not mean anything. I was in hopes he might become more interested in Miss Bengel, and perhaps he will, but they are both rather upon the brunette order and so physically at least are not good complements of each other. Well, well, I am anticipating far too much. I better wait till a week from today, before writing this paragraph and probably then there would be no occasion for it. (See later part of September 11th and 15th. See note added to September 10th in 1912, when I met Mr. Lucas in Soochow in 1907.)[71]

Went to bed 10 p.m. Took a carbolic soap bath, when I went out in the hall at about 10:30 p.m. to put out electric light, I saw out in the dining room Mr. Lucas and Miss Smithey engaged over some fruit.

We had a delightful service down upon the lower deck with the Chinese today. All the missionary party went down. We sang, then the Christian Chinese "Choung Sing" (to whom I was introduced when we first came on the ship by his Sunday school teacher) read a chapter from John in Chinese. The Rev. Taft then explained what had been read and made a few other remarks pointing them to our Saviour, Choung Sing interpreting. Rev. Wheeler also made short address, several pretty gospel songs were sung and we returned to the upper deck. I think it must have been very encouraging to Choung Sing and to the one or two other Christian Chinese that are in the steerage, if no more, but I hope

---

[71] Rosetta added on the diary written on September 10, 1912, "November 10th 1912—read again during the visit of Dr. and Mrs. O. E. Brown, I met Mr. Lucas in Soochow the time of the China Centenary Conference, he was druggist and the director's right hand helper in their hospital there, did evangelistic work too I suppose, but really likes medical evidently."
China Centenary Missionary Conference was held at Shanghai April 5 – May 7, 1907 to make it a celebration of the close of the first century of Protestant missionary work in China.

and pray it may be the means of opening the way to eternal life to more than one present this afternoon.

At 8 p.m., we had in the dining saloon, a service of song. The Rev. Tewksbury[72] also prayed. They sang till about 9:30. I then had a little run upon deck with the gals and returned for the night.

Monday, September 8, 1890

His compassions fail not. They are new every morning. Lam. iii.22,23

Another beautiful day: I arose, took a bath, dressed and came up on deck about an hour before breakfast—read my Bible lesson, and took a walk with Miss Bengel.

The sea is very calm today, scarcely a ripple. It seems as if it changed its hue every day—first it was green, then indigo blue, then a beautiful dark purplish blue, while today it is a real sky blue. It is so very smooth that one longs to get out in a rowboat upon it.

I cannot help thinking how very true at the present time my morning text is—surely His compassions fail not, and they are new every morning. How much I have to praise and love Him for bringing me thus far so safely and happily upon my journey.

---

[72] Rev. and Mrs. Elwood G. Tewksbury were appointed to China.

I have been trying to read something of Buddhism this morning sitting in my steamer chair upon the shady side of deck—but it is curious how lazy this placid voyage makes one feel. I can scarcely get up ambition enough to read anything that requires as much thought as that.

We are now 1200 miles out at sea—29° North Latitude 143° West Longitude. It is comfortable walking upon deck with no wraps, but a light wrap is needed when reclining in a steamer chair.

After lunch, the Purser took me to see the "Galley"[73] or kitchen where the food is cooked—it is not very large, so everything is pretty compact—it looked as clean and neat as kitchens usually do just after a meal. We looked into the baker's room where the bread and pie etc. are made—that looked well. Peeked into a large boiler of what looked like "Irish Stew," which was being prepared for the Chinese steerage – later I saw them eating it with their chopsticks. We also went to see two nice Jersey cows that go to freight, but the ship has the use of their milk for taking them. Sometime, not so soon after eating, the Purser said he would take me to see the pigpen, goose pen, and etc., all over the ship.

After dinner tonight, I walked a mile, 20 times around deck—started out with Miss Bengel then the Rev. Lucas joined us, and later Miss B. provoked me by leaving us. However, I managed to get on very well, though I can't say I felt just at my ease.

---

[73] The galley is the compartment of a ship where food is cooked and prepared.

Went to bed early. Slept till 7:30 a.m. We made for 299 miles today.

Tuesday, September 9, 1890

To him that ordereth his conversation aright will I show the salvation of God. Psa. I.23

> "If in our daily course, our mind
> Be set to hallow all we find,
> New treasures still, of countless price,
> God will provide for sacrifice."[74]

It is a little rougher this morning, but still pleasant. Could see a storm a long way off which cooled the atmosphere here somewhat. We are now getting down to 26° N. Latitude 148° West Longitude and it is very warm.

I came upon deck and had time to read my Bible lesson before breakfast. Saw some flying fish—they fly quite a long distance.

The Purser took up our tickets today. I started a letter home—we are to stop at Honolulu, so I can mail some letters there. I spent the rest of the forenoon mounting upon paper with thread and needle the specimens I gathered in Colorado, Utah, Wyoming, California, etc. Some of them look very pretty. I have quite a number from some places so can

---

[74] John Keble.

send some to a few of my Eastern friends whom I think would like them.

S.S. Orontes, the English vessel

3:30 p.m. A ship in sight—can see three sails peeping up beyond miles of water. It made quite a little excitement, some thinking it was a fleet of ships going the same way that we are, others thought they are coming our way, but now the conclusion is that it is a large sailing vessel crossing our path toward the north. She came within plain sight by 4 p.m. and she made a very pretty picture with all her sails up. She looked just like my ship puzzle that Frank gave me when I was a little girl, and by the way that reminds me that I didn't bring that. I wish I had it now for it had all the different parts of a ship named upon it and was very instructive, but I've forgotten it all now when I would enjoy it most. The strange vessel saluted ours first with a plain red flag, then she ran up four which our captain said after looking them up showed she was the *Orontes*, an English vessel. She was so near to us when she crossed our bow[75] that with a glass we could see the people upon the deck. It did seem too bad to see her moving farther and farther away from us without us stopping to shake hands even; but now she has gone almost—only a little spec upon the northeast horizon.

I commenced a letter home today, must write two more, I think before we reach Honolulu. We had made 311 miles at noon today—our best run yet. It is getting very warm. A number of the ship's officers and the cabin gentlemen had a game of cricket upon the lower deck today.

After dinner tonight, I took a short walk with Miss Smithey, and then we sat down and I led her into telling me how she came to take up Mission work, and she gave me a very complete an interesting account which raised her 88% in my estimation. She seems to be a very good sort of a girl after all, only she has always been used to doing just as she pleased—her parents being dead, and her older sister and brothers just shielding her and allowing her everything. She has been used to plenty of gentlemen company and is quite fond of it, so it is a very natural of her to behave as she has been doing upon the ship I expect. I think she means nothing by it, and believe she is a very good girl after all.

Went to bed 10 p.m. It is so warm I could have nothing over me but my thin muslin nightdress covered by my flannel wrapper, and I felt so enervated in the morning I hardly had ambition to get up.

---

[75] The bow is the forward part of the hull of a ship, the point that is usually most forward when the vessel is underway. The other end of the ship is the stern.

Wednesday, September 10, 1890

He that ploweth should plow in hope. I. Cor. ix.10

A beautiful morning—warm, but a nice breeze—we put up a sail to catch some of it to help us on our way.

At noon, some white birds said to be hawks were seen. The Purser tried to point them out to me, but I couldn't see them.

I wrote to Dr. H. this afternoon, will add a few more words to it and to my home letter tomorrow, and then I hope to post them at Honolulu. I also wrote to Dr. Meta Howard.

We had quite a hard shower this afternoon—it was rather pretty—could see where the raindrops made little pits in the water as they struck it, something as they do in dust. It cooled off the atmosphere nicely so that now it is quite comfortable if we are in the Torrid Zone.[76]

Made 312 miles today.

Just before dinner tonight, Miss Bengel and I were taking a "constitutional"[77] and I told her that tomorrow Mr. Livingstone would leave us at Honolulu and I overheard him ask the Purser who was to take his place at the table; and he told of some gentlemen, I didn't catch the name, who wished to—the Purser made no affirmation reply as far as I heard. Miss B. said she wished she could sit there: it turns out she

---

[76] Also known as Tropics.
[77] "Constitutional" means a walk or other mild exercise taken for the benefit of one's health.

doesn't like Rev. Lucas much, and as he is the only one at her table of our party she would like to come to ours. (Dr. Campbell sits at ours to which perhaps is some attraction.) So I said all right—we will ask the Purser at once and I think he will arrange it for us if we get to him before he promises anyone else, so we went and I told him we had a favor to ask of him. He said "granted." I then told him he said certainly she could sit there for dinner tomorrow night, but it would make it pretty hard for him to have a young lady upon either side he feared he would lose his appetite. Well if he will only lose his appetite for <u>wine</u> I shall be glad. I am going to hope that we may do him some little good. He needs it badly enough. After dinner he took my arm and very gallantly helped me up the stairs upon deck, found a comfortable chair with a footstool, and then excused himself for his after dinner cigar. Later, Miss Bengel and I were walking and he asked to join us, and spent most of the rest of the evening with us—Rev. Lucas and Miss Smithey enlivening us by their presence now and then.

How foolish of me to write all of this trash about people, but there isn't much else now. The sea and the steamer remained about the same and will for the rest of the time I expect. The people only change. Suppose I might better write nothing, but it is easier very often to pass the time this way than any other and perhaps sometimes it may amuse me to look it over, and then to burn it up.[78]

---

[78] Rosetta added later, "December 31st—I do find it amusing this last day of 1908, and am not ready to burn it up yet." Then she added 43

Went to bed 10 p.m. My urticaria or "flea bites" it looks more like now trouble me about the same. I do wish I could get the better of them.

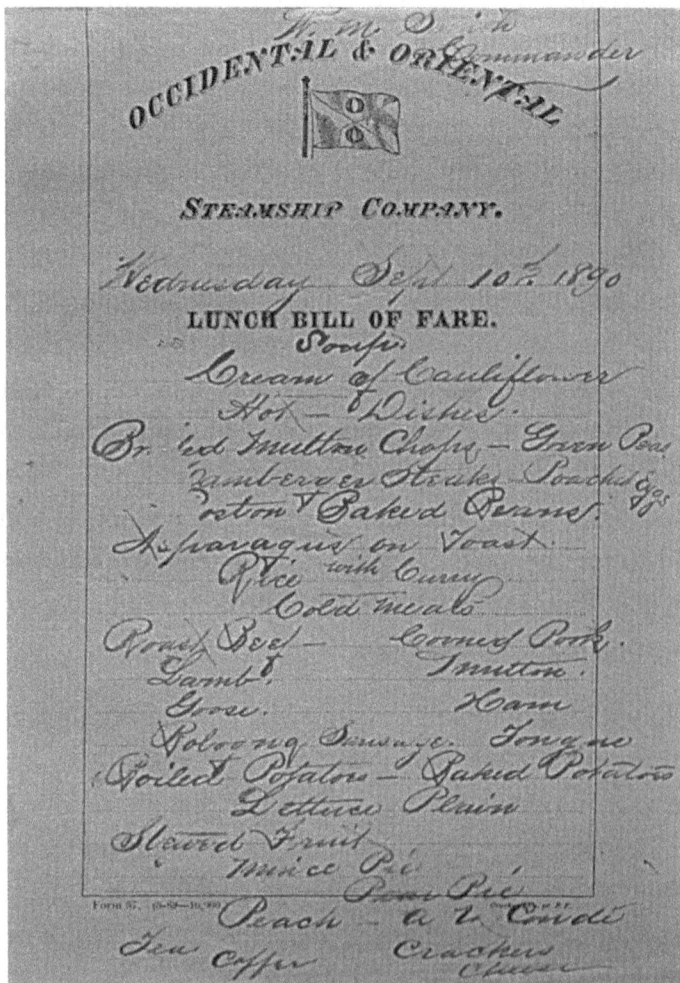

Bill of Fare for lunch, Wednesday, September 10, 1890

---

years later, "Ditto, February 1, 1933," 50 years later, "Ditto, January 15, 1940."

Thursday, September 11, 1890

We know that we have passed from death to life, because we love the brethren. I Jn. iii.14

One week ago today, we lost sight of land. Today, we sight it again for the first. I got up quite early to see the sunrise but was 10 minutes too late. It was 6 a.m. when I got upon deck, but though I didn't see the sunrise, a sailor pointed out the land (Hawaii probably) to me—it looks like a cloud upon our southeast Horizon. No one but a sailor would know it was land I think. I was the first lady to see it. Dr. Benn came up soon after and later others.

There is quite a breeze this morning and very pleasantly cool. I hardly feel warm enough without a wrap just now.

I took my salt water bath after breakfast and when I came upon deck, the Island "Oahu" upon which Honolulu is situated was just at our right—it seemed but 2 or 3 miles away but the captain said it was 10 [miles away]. It was very refreshing to see the steep cliffs, tall mountains and green valleys, after having seen nothing but the level Pacific for so long. We could make out with the field glass a sugar plantation with windmill, and buildings, also some small houses by the seaside. The mountains are peculiar. I don't know how to describe them but they are different from anything I ever saw.

We had lunch at 12 noon as we expected to anchor at 1 p.m., which we did about two miles out—the coral reefs are such that a large vessel like ours cannot get nearer. These reefs are said to be blue and their reflection at different depths of the water is what makes the most beautiful display of colors I ever saw, peacock blue sandwiched in between sky blue and a beautiful hue of green—at a distance you could notice the very line where one seemed to terminate and the other to begin.

Small boats mostly manned by native Hawaiians soon joined our ship. One small craft was loaded with bananas and sugar cane. The latter went off like hot cakes at 10 cents apiece among our Chinese steerage. They eat it as though very fond of it. Miss Richardson, one of the South Methodist gals bought a cane, and I had a taste of it—it is very juicy and very sweet.

We are to take on 300 Chinese steerage passengers here, and soon the first tug[79] load with their baggage made their appearance. There were several women dressed in the height of Chinese fashion, shining black hair done up with artificial flowers, bound feet, etc. Some of them could scarcely walk up the steps from the tug to the ship. Their feet were so useless—they had to depend upon their hands and the railing mostly. There are several children and some little babies. They all look clean and well dressed.

Most of our cabin passengers went off in small parties in the native boats to the city. I went with Dr. McCartney and wife and a Mrs. Smith who goes to live with a son, a dentist in Yokohama. We had two splendid oarsmen—the oldest one was an especially handsome muscular man, a good

---

[79] Tugboat.

specimen of the Malay type. They pulled their oars with a right good will and we overtook and passed a party that started out before us.

I have never been so surprised in my life as I am with this—Sandwich Island. I had thought the Sandwich Island to be the very "ends of the earth" and not place to be desired, and lo, I found it a very "garden of Eden." It seems like fairyland—one great Horticultural Hall with homes, stores and business places, street cars, telegraph, telephone, and every American convenience. The people speak English. The advertisements are in English. And no one could imagine that this intelligent Christian nation were savage cannibals less than 80 years ago. Here is an example of [what] Christianity can do. The native women here wear Mother Hubbard dresses altogether. They are very comfortable for this tropical climate. I saw some of them riding astride like a man. That is the style here I expect.

We were besieged the minute we landed by several white and some native to take a carriage and see the sights of the city. One white man wanted $15 for the four of us. He came down to six, but we went with a native who only charged us four dollars for 1½ hour ride and took us upon the principal streets, by fine residences, churches, school houses, etc. We saw the most beautiful lawns with tropical trees and flowers. The oleander grows like trees here—the most a beautiful red and some pure white. There were date palms, coconut trees, breadfruit, and whole orchards of bananas. Many flowers grow wild that we take much pain to cultivate.

Clockwise: "Date Palms, Orange tree, A leaf from a Date Palm, Orange grove, A home in an orange grove, Ripe dates."

"Residence Honolulu"

Everything was so beautiful and the air was delightful—
not so heated as I imagined it would be. The dust was laid
by street sprinklers. We drove by the Palace quite a modern
looking building, but very large and handsome of grey stone
mostly. The guards standing about dressed in white here
and there in the beautiful park surrounding the Palace. We
drove about the Public building, the house where the Prince
lived, and in upon the Queens Hospital grounds—the hospital and grounds are very fine. We then went to the other side
of town and saw the prison and fish ponds—the prisoners
were just returning in gangs now working upon the roads—
they were principally natives with a few white and Chinese.
Honolulu has its Chinatown—quite good quarters. Many
Chinamen seem to be doing splendid business—they have
meat markets, fruit markets, shops, tea and coffee restau-

rants, bakeries, and laundries of course. Saw several Chinese riding out in their carriages. We went into one fruit shop and the Chinese that kept it seemed bright as a new button. He spoke English well. I bought over one dozen bananas for 5 cents. I went into a dry goods store and bought me a traveling cap and a couple of neckties—the stores look much like those in our American cities. The whole city was one constant source of surprise to me at every turn. Oh, I am so thankful to the dear Father for bestowing this great privilege upon me. Honolulu is such an example of his might and power, and his exceeding great love—oh what may the love of God shed abroad in our hearts not do?

We secured the same oarsmen to take us back—they charged us $1 a piece crossing over, but a pants off of us went back for 50 cents-piece. Oh, but that was the grandest row I ever had in my life. Just think of—out upon the mighty Pacific in a common little row boat with but two oars!

For several days I've been wishing when I look at this calm ocean that I could get out in a boat upon it, but I didn't think I'd be so fortunate. In all this trip so far, He has made it better than all I had hoped. The sun went down behind the waters while we were upon them and it was a beautiful sight. The surge was lovely, and oh the waves that we would mount and go down over the other side. It was indeed the most enjoyable things that has occurred to me. I feel as though I would enjoy it for a long, long time. It was all too short back to the old ship again.

I got me a few specimens of wildflower and leaves to press.

Our party got back in time for dinner which was late— some of the others went to missionaries upon the island where we were all invited to go, and they had their dinner there, and didn't return till 9 o'clock. They had a most delightful time and brought back a bushel basket of fruit for us all.

After dinner, I was resting in my steamer chair upon deck when Rev. Lucas joined me. We passed the time quite pleasantly until 10 o'clock when I excused myself. I can't quite make him out. He seems quite careless, but he talks about my being transferred from Corea to China and some things like that which I don't want to hear if he means it, but he "fools" so much I can't be sure what he means and what he don't? He was talking about South Carolina his home and invited me to visit it someday. I asked him if he would be there, he said "perhaps we would come back together." I said "possible" but very impossible. His ways and talk remind me some of Mr. Hawkins.

Later I was with Mrs. Vogel upon deck when Dr. Campbell joined us. He certainly has most wonderful conversational powers—one can't help being entertained by him. It almost makes up for the cigarettes he smokes. I don't know why he comes and talks to me now and then, but I think because I am Miss Bengel's friend—Mistake – Miss Lanterman.

It was 2 a.m. before they got all the Chinese and their baggage aboard and we could start on our way again.

Friday, September 12, 1890

Pray for the peace of Jerusalem: they shall prosper that love thee. Ps. cxxii.6

"O make thy church, dear Saviour,
A lamp of purest gold,
To bear before the nations
Thy true light, as of old."[80]

This day has passed much as the others before we stopped at Honolulu. Some think that the trip will grow rather monotonous during the coming 12 or 14 days before we are due at Yokohama. But I don't believe I shall tire of it. I just think I would enjoy it for a year! Dr. Alba said if I could live out doors for a year or two he thought I might entirely eradicate my strumous difficulty, and I am sure a year upon the ocean would do me a great deal of good—and I should enjoy it more than camping. I just wish I could spend a year upon the Pacific—it is so delightful to me.[81]

I read about 15 pages of Buddhism today, but being up so late last night, I didn't feel very ambitious, and found it very comfortable (after a little talk with the Purser soon after lunch) to nap in my steamer chair for a couple of hours. Then I hunted up Miss Bengel and Dr. Stevenson, and we had some lemonade together, and then a little tramp upon deck.

After dinner tonight, I had a pleasant walk with Miss Bird[82], one of the Congregational girls. She has been at Ober-

---

[80] William Walsham How.
[81] Rosetta added later, "Time proved it did me great good."
[82] Susan R. Bird was appointed to China Inland Mission.

lin—a graduate I think—and I found she knows Dr. Thompson's people quite well and has seen him. She told me that he has such a lovely little mother. His father through disobeying an unjust law in slavery times in Missouri was put to prison at the time he was engaged to this delightful girl, and as his term was 12 years, he wished to release her from the engagement but she wouldn't be released, so after seven years, this law was repealed, and the faithful little woman was rewarded by the release of her lover. They were married and spent seven years in missionary work in Africa, then returned to America upon account of health. They have a fine family—one daughter a poetess, one a teacher in Oberlin, a son who has a splendid position for one so young as Professor in music, and then the doctor (See September 23rd).[83] They have also brought up some other children — brought two Africans home with them, and in many ways have been real missionaries all their lives. I had understood something of this from Dr. Thompson before, and I had judged that they were a very nice family. I always liked the doctor, could easily see he is what I like to call a "good man" and I am sure I was highly honored, much more so than I deserve to be, by what he expressed in such a beautiful but sincerely simple way, in a letter to me last April.

---

[83] Rosetta added later, "1912—The doctor and I were very good friends in New York City while I was in the Deaconess Home. We had many a Monday's excursion together: and we have always exchanged letters now and then. I met him and the good lady he married (some years after he went to Africa) at Battle Creek in 1910-11. It seemed so strange! Mrs. Jenkens was there too. He had grown quite old. I'd liked to have seen more of him."

Miss Bird is a real bright little person. I like her very well indeed. In fact, the majority, so I may say everyone, are people that one likes.[84]

Saturday, September 13, 1890

All things are of God. II Cor. v.18

"We give Thee but Thine own,
    Whate'er the gift may be;
All that we have is Thine alone,
    A trust, O Lord, from Thee."[85]

Pretty fair today with quite a stiff breeze, with the sails up we made 330 miles. Had a shower this afternoon.

I wrote 6 pages to Mrs. Jenkens, mostly about my visit to Honolulu: and I read quite a little of Buddhism. I think Buddha himself a very good person, and some of his sayings remind me of Solomon's Proverbs.

The Purser came while I was reading and sat down by me. We talked of school, of history and algebra, of our teachers, etc. Among other things he told me how when a child he never was so happy as when playing with nice-looking little

---

[84] Rosetta added later, "I heard that Miss Bird was killed in Boxer Movement." The Boxer Rebellion was an anti-imperialist uprising which took place in China in 1900. It was initiated by the Militia United in Righteousness (*Yihetuan*), known in English as the "Boxers," and was motivated by proto-nationalist sentiments and opposition to foreign imperialism and associated Christian missionary activity.
[85] William Walsham How,

girls, building play houses, making mud pies, etc. He was engaged to a pretty little girl when only 10 years old, and his heart was most broken by her death a little later. It reminded me of "Hazzy Dazzy" and "Daisy" in Mrs. Stowe's[86] *My Wife and I.* The wind was blowing so cool, and as it was nearly time for dinner, I excused myself and went down to get something warmer on. Mrs. Vogel, my room-mate, sat next to me, and when I went away the Purser took my chair and must have made himself agreeable, as usual, to her, for when she saw me next she said, "I think the Purser is such a nice gentleman." (He is only 25 I learned.)

After dinner, I took a short walk on deck and then sat down in my chair, and oh I felt so sleepy! I lowered the back of the chair and put out the foot rest and making myself comfortable, dozed away until nearly 10 p.m. Then hearing music down in the Saloon, I went down and heard Chief Engineer Allan sing several pretty songs, Rev. Tewksbury playing the piano. A copy of Nellie Bly's[87] around the world in 72 days lay on the table near me so I took occasion to glance it over quite thoroughly—it is very readable. She crossed the Pacific in <u>this</u> steamship, the "Oceanic" and her description of Captain Smith and some of the other officers is very good, as is that also of the vessel, the Chinese and Japanese servants, sailors, etc.

---

[86] Harriet Beecher Stowe, author of *Uncle Tom's Cabin.*
[87] Nellie Bly (1864 –1922) was the pen name of American journalist Elizabeth Jane Cochrane. She was a ground-breaking reporter known for a record-breaking trip around the world in 72 days.

Sunday, September 14, 1890

Who crowneth thee with loving kindness and tender mercies. Ps. Ciii.4

"Father and Friend! Thy light, Thy love,
    Beaming through all Thy works we see;
Thy glory gilds the heaven above,
    And all the earth is full of Thee."[88]

We had such a nice Service upon deck this morning. The steamer bell was rung so it sounded like church bells and we all gathered upon the Port[89] side of deck. Rev. Greenwood conducted the Episcopal service. Then Rev. Wheeler gave us an address the theme of which was inventions, basing his remarks upon Isaiah iii. 3.

The sea is very smooth again today. Not a white-cap to be seen, except in the wake of the vessel.

At 3 p.m., the majority of the missionary party with a few others met in the Saloon to study the Sunday school lesson together. It was the parable of the 10 pounds, one given to each of 10 servants.[90] There were diverse opinions but to mind the best explanation was something like this. The one pound that were given to each with the order to "occupy" or to traffic till I come represents the regenerate spirit which is a common gift to all who will accept it. The man who

---

[88] John Bowring.
[89] Port and starboard refer to the left and right sides of the ship, respectively.
[90] The Parable of the Ten Minas. Luke 19:11-27.

gained 5 pounds was probably as faithful as the one who gained 10 pounds, but he didn't have the capacity or the talents illustrated in the other parable to do quite so well. Each received the plaudit "well done." It is not "be thou successful," but "be thou faithful" as I have heard Mrs. Dickinson say many times. The man who laid away his gift in a napkin making no use of it lost it just as we would lose in time any faculty that is never used. Oh, I pray that I may be <u>faithful</u> and not mind about the success, which however is generally quite sure to follow faithfulness, but that does not rest with us. "Be thou faithful."

At 5 p.m., we went down to the Chinese [Service]. Choung Sing prayed in Chinese, and then another Christian Chinese, Fook King, addressed the Chinese, after singing another song the meeting closed. Quite a number of the Chinese and their children who came from Honolulu took part in the singing. One little boy of about 10 or 12 shared my book, and he sang out right vigorously.

We didn't have any service after dinner this evening. I was upon deck until nearly 11 p.m. The air was so delicious. I hated to go down into my state-room. I enjoyed it alone the most of the time, just largely watching some of the other passengers. Dr. Campbell and Miss Lanterman were near me, and she was trying to get him to do less smoking, but I fear she has a hard case on her hands. By and by, Rev. Lucas came and talked to me awhile and then I said good night and went to bed.

Monday, September 15, 1890

He hath made us accepted in the beloved. Eph. i.6

"If our love were but more simple,

We should take Him at His word;

And our lives would be all sunshine

In the sweetness of our Lord."[91]

We are now 28° North Latitude 176° West Longitude. Only made 299 miles from noon yesterday to noon today. Made 321 miles the day before. The sea is still smooth.

Had a Bible class 10 a.m. Prof. Wyckoff led it. Are going to have one every morning now.

I finished reading about Buddhism in my *Error's Chains: How Forged and Broken*.[92]

After dinner this evening, I joined the Tewksbury circle and enjoyed a game upon geography. Later Miss Smithey, Rev. Lucas and myself had a little lunch of fruit and candy, and a lot of fun over some of Reverend's remarks. "Mind you, I don't say that the doctor shall be Mrs. Ben Lucas."

---

[91] Frederick W. Faber.

[92] *Error's Chains: How Forged and Broken*. A complete, graphic, and comparative history of the many strange beliefs, superstitious practices, domestic peculiarities, sacred writings, systems of Philosophy, legends and traditions, customs and habits of mankind throughout the world, ancient and modern. By Frank S. Dobbins, 1883.

Tonight (Monday the 16th), we will go to bed and awake Wednesday the 17th. What becomes of the lost day? Can it ever be made up?[93]

Tuesday, September 16, 1890

Lost!

Wednesday, September 17, 1890

They that sow in tears shall reap in joy. Ps. cxxvi. 5

"There is a day of sunny rest
    For every dark and troubled night;
And grief may bide an evening guest,
    But joy shall come with early light.

For God hath marked each sorrowing day
    And numbered every secret tear,
And heaven's long age of bliss shall pay
    For all his children suffer here."[94]

Well, and here is a change sure, high winds and a rough sea. Much cooler. The old ship pitches and tosses quite a great deal and a number of the passengers feel seasick again.

I studied the Bible lesson with Miss Bengel a little while, and then I went with the Purser all over the vessel—we

---

[93] Rosetta answered herself later, "Yes, when we return and get the extra day!"

[94] William Cullen Bryant (1794–1878)

were nearly 2 hours. Went out to the butcher shop—a sheep that had just been dressed was hanging up. Saw the great wheel and chain that turns the rudder[95]—also the engine that does this guided by those little turns the Pilot makes in the wheel house. Then we went to see the great engine that propels the vessel—climbed down long iron ladders to the very bottom and watched the massive thing work. The engineer gave us some clean tow to hold in our palms when we took hold of the greasy iron railings. He took great pride in showing us all about the engine, and the dynamo that makes the electric light. Then he piloted us into the furnace room. Here at this side, there is a man at each furnace door who attends to taking out the ashes. They opened one door for me to look in, but I didn't care to look long—it was such a blazing blinding heat. The engineer then took a torch and stooping down we followed him between two furnaces in sort of a tunnel to the other side where the coal is shoveled in 60 tons a day! Saw great black rooms that had been emptied of coal, and others still full, enough to last us to Yokohama where they fill up again I believe. My! But I never imagined there was such a place on this vessel. I've not realized its size before—428 x 50 x 38 and 25 feet underwater. This place seemed like going down into a coal mine in the very lowly of the earth instead it being on a ship out in the Pacific. We climbed up and up out of this place into day light once more and went over to the bow of the vessel—passed the European steerage—quite a lot of Chinese on that side now. Then we saw the cages of chickens, pens of pigs, and

---

[95] A rudder is a primary control surface used to steer a ship.

there is still quite a flock of sheep. Here I saw the great chain to which the anchor is fastened.

I think I know a little more now what a "steamship" means than I did before, but there is a great deal more I'd like to understand about it.

Thursday, September 18, 1890

Godliness with contentment is great gain. I Tim. vi.6

> "Meekly upon His will to wait
> In little things as well as great,
> Contented in our lot to rest,
> 'Tis thus the Christian serves Him best."[96]

A fine day. The sea is quiet again. Made 310 miles. It is quite warm still.

I nearly finished reading Edward Bellamy's *Looking Backward*,[97] a tale of the year 2000. There are some wonderful ideas in it; and it does look as the world would be almost perfect if we could have the arrangement of everything as pictured in that book—and perhaps it will come? I would like to help it.

We had a hard rain this evening. It broke up a game of "I spy," which 7 or 8 of our missionary party were playing upon deck, so we went below into the dining saloon and

---

[96] J. S. B. Monsell.
[97] *Looking Backward* is Edward Bellamy's utopian novel,.

joined by 10 or 12 others played "Musical Mice," "Foolish Questions and Silly Answers." Then Chief Engineer Allen came in and introduced "Boston Change," which we played till 10:30 p.m. Just think of missionaries playing children's games. Well I'm sure I still feel a child at heart tho' tomorrow I will be a quarter of a century old!

Got to bed before 11 p.m. and slept straight through till 7:30 a.m.

Friday, September 19, 1890
Tuesday, September 19, 1865

The God of all grace...make you perfect, stablish, strengthen, settle you. I Pet. v.10

A calm beautiful morning. It is my 25th birthday. I wonder if they remember it at home? It makes me feel a wee bit sad this morning to think I must not only spend this birthday upon the Briny deep[98], but that if I should live to see four or five returns of the day they must also be spent among strangers in a strange land. But the dear Heavenly Father is with me here upon His mighty Ocean and He will surely be with me upon the other side. How exceedingly kind He has been to me all my life long.

> I will bring the blind by a way that they knew not; I will lead them in paths that they have not known: I will make darkness light before them, and crooked

---

[98] Deep blue sea.

things straight. These things will I do unto them, and not forsake them. Isa. xlii. 16

At noon today, we were in North Latitude 33° and East Longitude 166°, having made 324 miles since yesterday.

Rev. Wheeler led the Bible class today. The subject was I Cor. xiii. A number of quotations were made from Prof. Drummond's *Greatest Things in the World* and it was talked of at the table this morning, so I took occasion to ask the Purser if he had ever read it. He wanted to know "what is it"—"the almighty dollar" "or your best girl"? I told him he must read it and find out—so after Bible class, I took my copy to his desk where he was working over piles of papers, and said that he might read it at his leisure. I do hope it may prove a little help in the right direction.

I finished *Looking Backward* and began Count Tolstoy's *My Religion*,[99] which I think I am going to like. I bought upon the cars going from Chicago to Omaha Tolstoy's *Kreutzer Sonata*,[100] a book which I had not happened to have heard of before though I believe there had been a great deal said

---

[99] Count Tolstoy's *What I Believe* (1884) was also published in English as *My religion* and *My Faith*.

[100] *The Kreutzer Sonata* by Leo Tolstoy is a novella named after Beethoven's Kreutzer Sonata, published in 1889. The Russian authorities promptly censored the novella. In 1890, when it became obvious in Europe that *The Kreutzer Sonata* would not be published in Russia, the Bibliographic Office in Berlin published the story in four languages – Russian, German, French and English simultaneously. At least two other different English translations were published in 1890 simultaneously in England and America.

against it, and Comstock[101] had put a stop to it being sent through the mails, etc. But glancing it over and noticing some things that interested me and seeing it was by Tolstoy, I purchased it—and I am glad I did, for it seems to me to be <u>a book written with pure motives</u>, and I should think it might do good if people, young men especially, would but <u>take warning from</u> it—it certainly teaches "Social Purity" by showing to its black end what the lack of Social Purity brings about. I wonder what <u>a man</u> would say about this book?—not being sure about the propriety of speaking of it, I have never asked anyone's opinion of Tolstoy's *Kreutzer Sonata*.

A very pleasant surprise was planned for me by Dr. Stevenson, the Misses Bengel, Richardson, and Smithey and Mrs. McCartney. We were all invited to No. 25 at 9:30 p.m. and there they had told the Steward that it was my birthday and he had ordered a lovely great large cake baked, and covered with the prettiest frosting, and there were nuts and raisins, and apples and lemonade. So my birthday upon the *Oceanic* ended right, merrily.

---

[101] Anthony Comstock (1844-1915) was a U.S. Postal Inspector and politician, who created the New York Society for the Suppression of Vice in 1873 and successfully passed the Comstock Law, which made the delivery of "obscene, lewd, or lascivius" material by U.S. mail or by other modes of transportation illegal. The tariff laws giving customs clerks the right of censorship marked Tolstoy's *Kreutzer Sonata* an obscene literature; therefore, further import and distribution of this book in the U.S. was prohibited.

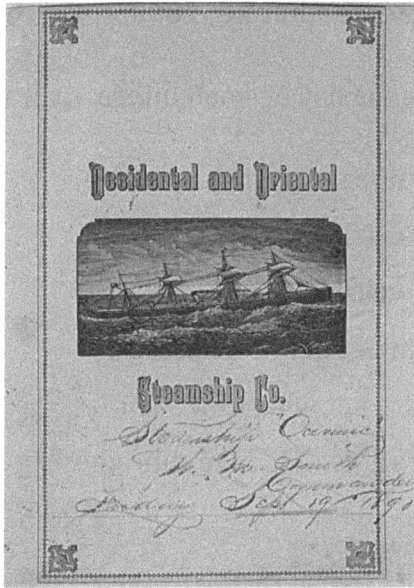

I walked for 40 minutes before dinner tonight—about 2½ miles surely, and I was too tired to enjoy the "Boston Change," which a great many played tonight.

Bill of Fare, Friday, September 19, 1890

Saturday, September 20, 1890

Despise not the day of small things. Zach. iv.10

"A smile of hope from those we love,

May be an angel from above,

A whisper welcome in our ears,

But as the music of the spheres;

Oh, trifles are not what they seem,

But nature's voice and love supreme."[102]

The Bible lesson (Col. I) was conducted by the Rev. Lucas this morning. It is still warmer today. I took a salt water bath this afternoon, and put on a cool dress, and felt more comfortable then.

The Purser returned Drummond's *The Greatest Thing in the World*, said he found it very readable.

Didn't make much progress in *My Religion* today. Hardly know what I have been doing all day. Oh yes, after Bible class this morning, I wrote to Dr. Hall. I can read some tomorrow, but after that, I shall have to write I think if we get in Yokohama Wednesday morning. I must write home, and

---

[102] George Linnaeus Banks.

I should write to Mrs. Skidmore. Then there are several letters I came across in my trunk this afternoon that I received just before leaving home and planned to answer upon the ship board, and forgot all about till now.

Sunday, September 21, 1890

Lord, what wilt Thou have me to do?[103] Acts ix.6

"Father, I wait Thy daily will,
Thou shalt divide my portion still;
Grant me on earth what seems Thee best,
Till death and heaven reveal the rest."[104]

Another beautiful Sabbath morning, my third upon shipboard. I wonder where I shall be next Sunday.

Made 310 miles today, are now 35° North Latitude and 154° East Longitude.

Rev. Taft conducted the Episcopal service, and Rev. Greenwood preached from Isaiah.

---

[103] This day's Bible verse, "Lord, what wilt Thou have me to do?" is from the KJV. This expression is slightly different in the NIV translation, which is written as, "You will be told what you must do." The Korean Bible translated from the NIV, thus follows the latter translation.
[104] Isaac Watts.

Everyone liked the sermon very much. It was real good for us. One illustration in particular pleased me. There is a fine fresco in the dome of a building in Rome, but it tires one very much to hold back his head long enough to see it all he would like so he makes use of a mirror which is set at such an angle as to reflect the fresco perfectly. It is thus with the Father—we cannot behold Him in our natural strength, but we can see Him reflected in the person of His Son, our Lord and Savior.

He spoke very touchingly of the many pleasant acquaintances formed in our long voyage, which is now approaching its close when we must part each to go his way to pursue his particular vocation in life, and he hoped that though we might not meet again in this life that not one who heard his voice would miss being gathered home in the arms of the great All Father by and by.

We had a nice service with the Chinese at 5 p.m. Rev. Tewksbury conducting it. Choung Sing made quite a lengthy address in Chinese, which judging from his expression and that upon the faces of the Chinese must have been pretty good—droll at times because they laughed.

Monday, September 23, 1890[105]

Yield yourselves unto God. Rom. vi.13

It is much rougher today. Have to have the boxing about our plates at the table, and then things slide around considerable. It is a very warm, 80°, but so humid that it seems 90°. We are 35° North 147° East.

After Bible class, I wrote to Mrs. Skidmore. She asked me to write to her several times upon my way, and I've not written but once before. After lunch, I wrote a short letter to Dr. Thompson. I didn't know hardly whether I ought to answer his last letter or not, but after meeting Miss Bird I thought it would be rather nice to write and tell him of her, and a little something of my trip so far. It will be all right I think.[106]

About 4 p.m., I went down to my state-room and packed my steamer trunk. It was very hot work. We made 323 miles today.

The vessel rocked us like a cradle tonight and I enjoyed it!

---

[105] The date of this diary is likely Monday, September 22, 1890. The steamer arrived in Yokohama on Tuesday, September 23, 1890 and Rosetta had the "last dinner upon board the Oceanic" on Tuesday evening as shown on the Bill of Fare.

[106] Rosetta added later, "It proved so."

Tuesday, September 24, 1890[107]

Return, ye backsliding children, and I will heal your backslidings. Jer. iii.22

Still rough. Had a real hard shower before breakfast. It is so warm and moist that it takes the starch quite out of one.

We expect to anchor off Yokohama sometime tonight.

Had our last Bible lesson upon deck, conducted by Rev. Headland.

I wrote to Uncle Robert and Cousin Charley this afternoon. While I was writing, Japanese fishing smacks came in sight and the coast of Niphon seemed not far away. It reminds one of the coast of Oahu, but is hardly as pretty I think.

About 6 p.m., the sacred Mount Fuji came in sight—its cone-shaped top covered with clouds and at sunset we had the most beautiful picture I think I ever saw, a line of dark mountains in the foreground reaching down to the sea, above these a golden sky and misty mountains farther beyond with this golden glow in front while above them and surrounding the top of Fuji were clouds of different hues and tints of red just as the sun dropped down below the horizon. For nearly a half hour as the colors became darker

---

[107] The date of this diary is likely Tuesday, September 23, 1890.

or changed here and there, the picture seemed yet so beautiful that I could hardly tell at what time I liked it best, and I cannot undertake to find words to at all do justice to its magnificence at any time.

"Fujiyama reigns over the whole life of Japanese, visible to nearly the whole of the country from one capital to the other. It is one of the most sacred of mountains: one of the greatest pilgrimage places: and it is incomparably beautiful: a vast pyramid, with palm leaf curves rising from the very sea, and spurning all buttressing from the surrounding mountains. It towers for the best part of the year in a priestly vestment of snow—the monarch of truncated cones, the Parthenon of volcanoes."[108] Height 12,000.

We had a grand dinner tonight—our last upon the *Oceanic*. I enclose a bill of fare. The oysters were splendid. We had them every two or three days, five large fresh Baltimore

---

[108] This is hand-written information by Rosetta on the back of the Mt. Fuji photo. *Queer Things About Japan,* p320.

oysters—think of it away out here in the Eastern hemisphere—they are kept frozen all the time until wanted upon the table. The tables looked very pretty indeed—the artistic way in which our napkins were folded in many various fan-like forms standing up in the glasses, the celery, the handsomely frosted cake, the "Jelly an Kirsch" all lent something to the pleasing effect of the whole.

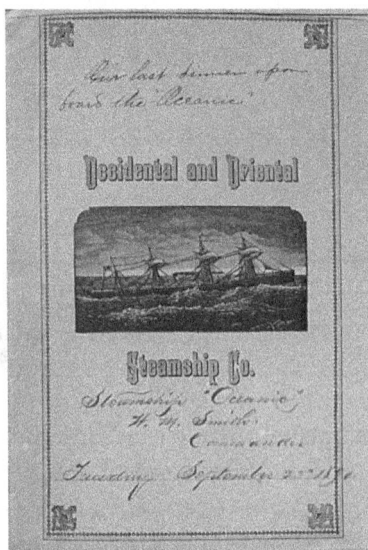

The last dinner menu upon board the S.S. Oceanic, September 23, 1890

Soon after dinner, we anchored off Yokohama. Some went ashore of the "Globe trotters," and a few others, but most of the missionary party waited till morning. We had a quiet night of it. I took my last ocean bath and went to bed 10 p.m.

I find I have nearly written this book full, so that if I continue my scribbling, I will have to take up "No. 2." I will do that tomorrow I think—my first day on land in the Eastern Hemisphere, so "goodbye" to "No. 1."

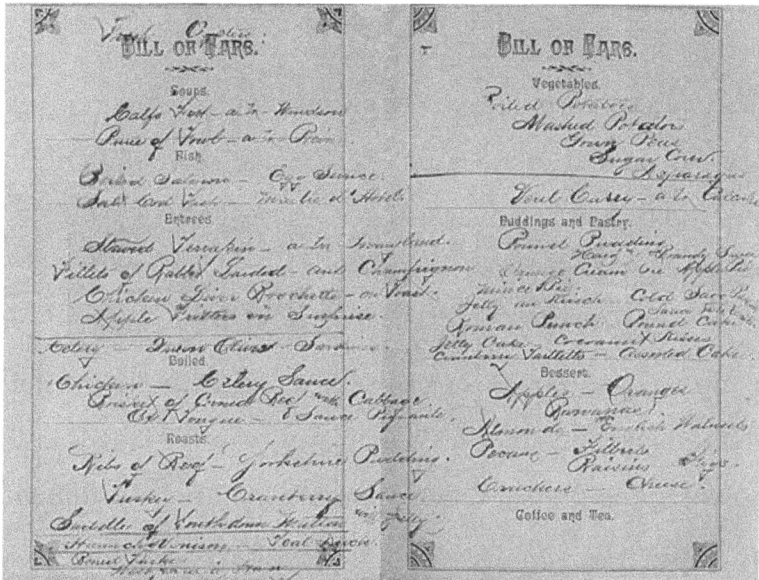

Bill of Fare, Tuesday, September 23, 1890

"He that good thinketh good may do,

And God will help him thereunto;

For was never good work wrought

Without beginning of good thought."

Many think they are in love, When in fact they are only idle.
—Imlac in *Rasselas*[109]

"Reverence the highest, have patience with the lowest. Let this day's performance of the meanest duty be thy religion. Are the stars too distant, pick up the pebble that lies at thy feet and from it learn the all."—Margaret Fuller Ossoli[107]

"I am obliged to consider as sacred and absolute the sole and unique union by which man is once for all indissolubly bound to the first woman with whom he has been united."
—Tolstoy[108]

"Not myself, but the truth that in life I have spoken,
Not myself, but the seed that in life I have sown,
Shall pass on to ages,—all about me forgotten,
Save the truth I have spoken, the things I have done."
—Horatius Bonar[109]

[106, 107, 108, 109] Rosetta had added these four poems and quotations for her September 19, 1890 diary. Whenever she felt the need to supplement the content of her diary, Rosetta usually filled the empty spaces of the pages designated to that specific diary; however, on this very day of her 25th birthday, she probably had quite a bit to add and thus chose to pen them down at the end of the book.

Timeline of Dr. Rosetta Sherwood Hall
(1865 – 1951)

1865	9.19	Born in Liberty, New York
		Mother: Phoebe Gildersleeve Sherwood
		Father: Rosevelt Rensler Sherwood
1876		Graduates from Chestnut Ridge Primary School
1880		Graduates from Liberty Normal Institute
1881	9	Enters Liberty Normal Institute's "Teacher's Class"
	10	Obtains Second Grade Teacher's Certificate[110]
1882	2.6	Transfers to Montgomery Union School, following her former professor Mr. Reuben Fraser[111], newly appointed Principal of the school
	4	Graduates from Montgomery Union School
	5.1	Starts teaching at Huntington District School
	9.6	Enters the Oswego State Normal School

---

[110] By the time Rosetta was teaching, a first grade certificate was good for 2 years, a second grade certificate good for eighteen months, and third grade certificate good for 12 months.

[111] Professor Reuben Fraser was Principal of the Liberty Normal Institute when Rosetta entered the school, but when the Montgomery Academy merged with a public school in 1882 and became the Montgomery Union School, he took the position of Principal.

Diary of Dr. Rosetta Hall 1890

1883		Graduates from the Oswego State Normal School; obtains a First Grade Teacher's Certificate; teaches at Bethel District School
1884		Teaches at Chestnut Ridge School, Sullivan County, New York
1886		Enters the Woman's Medical College of Pennsylvania
1889	3.14	Graduates from the Woman's Medical College of Pennsylvania Interns at the Nursery and Children's Hospital, Staten Island
	11	Works as a physician for the New York Deaconess Home Begins medical missionary work in Hell's Kitchen in New York City; meets her future husband Rev. William James Hall, M.D. (b. January 16, 1860, Glen Buell, Ontario, Canada), who is in charge of the medical missionary work in the slums of New York
1890	8.21	Leaves Liberty, New York for Korea as a medical missionary, under the auspices of the Woman's Foreign Missionary Society of the Methodist Episcopal Church
	9.4	Boards the *S.S. Oceanic* in San Francisco
	9.24	Arrives in Yokohama
	10.10	Arrives in Pusan, Korea

Diary of Dr. Rosetta Hall 1890

	10.13	Arrives in Chemulpo, Korea
	10.14	Arrives in Seoul
	10.15	Starts medical work at Po Ku No Kwan, the firs Woman's Hospital and Dispensary established by the Methodist Episcopal Mission
	10.24	Selects two girls from the Ehwa-Haktang Mission School, O Waka San and Chom Tong Kim, for medical assistance training
1891	1.25	Chom-Tong is baptized as "Esther"
	1	Starts teaching physiology to five girls: Esther, O Waka San, Susanna, Pong Sun ("Mary Sparks Wheeler"), and Annie
	8.21	Travels to Chefoo, China, with Miss Bengel
	12.15	William James Hall arrives in Korea (Pusan) as a medical missionary for the Methodist Episcopal Church
1892	3	William goes on a country trip with George Heber Jones; visits Pyongyang for the first time
	6.27	Rosetta marries William James Hall
	7	Returns to Seoul from a honeymoon in Chefoo

Diary of Dr. Rosetta Hall 1890

	9	William is appointed to Pyongyang; Rosetta is appointed to Seoul
1893	3.15	Opens the East Gate Dispensary (Baldwin Dispensary) in Seoul
	5.24	Esther Kim marries Yousan Pak
	11.10	Rosetta and William's first son Sherwood is born in Seoul
1894	5.8	The Hall family arrives in Pyongyang with Esther and Yousan; begins medical work; begins instruction of the blind girl Pong-Nae O
	6.6	Evacuates to Seoul due to persecution
	8.1	Sino-Japanese War begins
	10.1	William leaves for Pyongyang
	11.19	William returns to Seoul, sick with typhus fever
	11.24	William dies
	12.10	Rosetta departs from Chemulpo to America with her son Sherwood and Esther and Yousan
	12.16	Arrives in Nagasaki
	12.18	Arrives in Kobe

Diary of Dr. Rosetta Hall 1890

	12.21	Boards the *S.S. China* in Yokohama for San Francisco
1895	1.6	Arrives in San Francisco
	1.14	Arrives in Liberty, New York
	1.18	Gives birth to Edith Margaret in Liberty, New York
	2	Esther Pak enters the Liberty Union School; Yousan works at the Sherwood Farm
	4	Begins a biography of her late husband and fundraises for the establishment of the Hall Memorial Hospital in Pyong-yang
	6.27	Rosetta's father Rosevelt R. Sherwood dies
	8	Rosetta visits her husband's family in Glen Buell, Ontario with her children and Esther and Yousan
	9	Esther Pak enters the Nursery and Children's Hospital of New York City; also studies for admission into the medical school
	10	Rosetta attends the Annual Meeting of the New York Branch of the Woman's Foreign Missionary Society (W.F.M.S.) in Brooklyn, October 16-18; visits Esther Pak at the hospital
1896	2	Visits New York and Middletown

	4	Attends a conference for the International Medical Missionary Society (I.M.S.S.), New York City
	5	Moves residence to 121 E. 45th Street with children and Yousan
	6	Moves into the New York Deaconess Home for work; sends children back to Liberty; Yousan takes a new job for the family of Rev. A.B. Sanford in New York
	6.22	Begins work at the New York Deaconess Home; works as the examining physician for the Christian Herald Fresh-Air Children Summer Camp at Mt. Lawn, Nyack until September
	9	Esther Pak enters the Baltimore Woman's Medical College
	9.28	Rosetta works for the International Medical Missionary Society; moves back into 121 E. 45th Street residence with children
	10.28	Attends the General Executive meeting for the W.F.M.S. at Rochester, New York
1897	2.1	Establishment of the Hall Memorial Hospital in Pyongyang; Sherwood attends kindergarten until March
	5.20	Closes her work for I.M.M.S. at the Deaconess Home; decides to return to Korea
	5.22-30	Visits Esther Pak in Baltimore

Diary of Dr. Rosetta Hall 1890

5.31   Arrives in Liberty, New York; finishes manuscripts of her husband's biography; Yousan also returns to Liberty to depart for Korea

8   Publishes *The Life of Rev. William James Hall, M.D.*
        Yousan decides not to return to Korea and gets a new job at Mrs. Adgate's house, near the Sherwood farm

9.6   Rosetta leaves Liberty for Korea with Sherwood and Edith Margaret; visits husband's family in Glen Buell, Ontario enroute to Korea

10.11   Boards the *S.S. Empress of India* in Vancouver

11.10   Arrives in Chemulpo

        Makes the first embossed book for the blind of Korea, pricked on oiled Korean mulberry paper by hand

1898   4.29   Leaves Seoul to start work in Pyongyang

        5.1   Arrives in Pyongyang

        5.23   Edith Margaret dies of dysentery

        6.18   Opens the Women's Dispensary of Extended Grace in Pyongyang, as well as the Mother-Baby Clinic and the School for the Blind

1899   5   Attends the Annual Meeting in Seoul; embarks on a building project of the Edith Margaret Children's Wards

Diary of Dr. Rosetta Hall 1890

1900	1	The School for the Blind is built
	4.28	Yousan Pak dies in Baltimore of tuberculosis
	5.5	Rosetta's mother Phoebe G. Sherwood dies
	5	Esther Pak receives M.D. degree
	10	Esther Pak arrives in Korea
1901	3	Due to overwork, Rosetta recuperates in Chemulpo and Seoul
	5	Attends Annual Meeting in Seoul
	6.7	Departs for America with Sherwood
	6.22	Boards the *S.S. Nippon Maru* in Yokohama
	7.7	Arrives in San Francisco
	7	Arrives in Castile, New York
	8	Enters the Castile Sanatorium and stays for 8 months
	10	Attends the New York Branch Annual Meeting
1902	4.5	Discharged from the Sanatorium; moves to Brother Charles' home
	8.14	Leaves Liberty for Korea (via Europe)

Diary of Dr. Rosetta Hall 1890

	8.25	Visits husband's family in Canada for one week
	9.2	Boards the *S.S. St. Paul* in New York
	9.10	Arrives in London
	10.16	Boards the *S.S. Glen Logan* from Swansea to Batúm
1903	3.18	Arrives in Seoul, Korea
		Works at the Women's Hospital of Extended Grace in Pyongyang with Esther Pak
1906	11	The Women's Hospital of Extended Grace in Pyongyang is burnt down
1908	9	The new Women's Hospital of Extended Grace in Pyongyang is built
		Sherwood completes the eighth grade at Pyongyang Foreign School and enters the Chefoo Boarding School
1909		Rosetta opens the Pyongyang School for the Deaf
1910	4.13	Esther Pak dies of tuberculosis
	6	Rosetta attends the Edinburgh World Missionary Conference as a delegate from Korea, and then takes a furlough in America
1911	4	Sherwood enrolls at the Mount Hermon School in Massachusetts

Diary of Dr. Rosetta Hall 1890

		Rosetta completes her furlough and returns to Korea
1912	3	Starts a Medical Training Class in Pyongyang with Mary Cutler, M.D.
1914	8	Enrolls three female students as auditors at the Government Medical School in Seoul: Soo-Kyong Ahn, Hae-Ji Kim, and Young-Heung Kim
		The First Annual Convention on the Education of the Blind And Deaf of the Far East is held in Pyongyang, August 11-14
1915		Sherwood enters Mount Union College in Alliance, Ohio
1917		Rosetta moves to Seoul; works at the East Gate Woman's Hospital and Dispensary
1918		Takes a furlough; works as a physician for the Board of Health in Philadelphia; Sherwood is engaged to Marian Bottomley
		The three female students at the Government School obtain medical licenses
1920		Rosetta starts a Woman's Medical Training Class in Seoul
	9	Marian Bottomley enters the Woman's Medical College of Pennsylvania
1921		Rosetta serves as the director of the East Gate Woman's Hospital and Dispensary
		Opens a Women's Hospital in Chemulpo

Diary of Dr. Rosetta Hall 1890

1922	6.21	Sherwood and Marian Bottomley are married in Ohio
1923		Sherwood graduates from the Medical College at the University of Toronto
1924	6	Marian Bottomley graduates from the Woman's Medical College of Pennsylvania
1925	8.15	Sherwood and his wife leave for Korea
1927	2.18	Rosetta's grandson William James Hall is born
1928	9.4	The Woman's Medical Training Class in Seoul becomes the Kyong-Sung Woman's Medical Institute
	10.28	Sherwood opens the Haiju School of Hygiene for the Tuberculosis
1932	10.8	Second grandson Joseph Keightley is born
	12.3	Sherwood prints the first Christmas Seal (1932-1933) in Korea
1933	9.23	The Haiju Sanatorium dedicates its chapel to Rosetta
	11	The Woman's Medical Institute graduates its first students
	11.25	Retires from the mission field; returns to America to take care of Brother Frank Sherwood in Groversville, New York
1934	9.12	Granddaughter Phyllis Marian is born

1936		Opens a medical practice in Groversville, New York
1938		Returns to Liberty and opens a medical practice
1943		Retires from medicine; moves to the Bancroft-Taylor Rest Home in Ocean Grove, New Jersey
1951	4.5	Dies in Ocean Grove, New Jersey. Ashes are interred at Yanghwajin Foreign Missionary Cemetery in Seoul

Publications

The Life of Rev. William James Hall, M.D., Medical Missionary to the Slums of New York, Press of Easton and Mains, New York, August 1897.

"A Country Trip in Korea," *The Gospel in All Lands*, Vol. 21, November 1900, 494-497.

"Early Medical Work for Women in Korea,"*Women's Missionary Friend*, Vol. 13, December 1902.

"The Clocke Class for Blind Girls," *Korea Mission Field*, Vol. 11, No. 1, September 1905 – January 1907.

"Women's Medical Work, Pyeng Yang," *Korea Mission Field*, Vol. 5, No. 7, July 1909.

"Mrs. Esther Kim Pak, M.D.: Korea's First Woman Doctor," Woman's Foreign Missionary Society, Methodist Episcopal Church, Publication Office, Boston, Massachusetts, c. 1910.

"The Deaf and Blind in Korea," *The Christian Herald*, May 1911.

"The Use of White Clothes the Year Round," *Korea Mission Field*, Vol. 8, No. 8, August 1912.

"Glimpses of Women's Medical Work in Korea," *Women's Work in the Far East*, December 1913.

"Medical Needs of Korean Women," *China Medical Journal*, September 1915.

Diary of Dr. Rosetta Hall 1890

"Department for Blind and Deaf, Pyeng Yang," *Korea Mission Field*, Vol. 11, No. 1, December 1915.

"Pioneer Mission of Korean Native Costumes," *China Medical Journal*, March 1916.

"Gynecological Dispensary in Korea," *China Medical Journal*, September 1916.

"A 'Battalion of Life' Wanted for Chosen," *Woman's Work: A Foreign Mission Magazine*, 1919, p153-155.

"Women Physicians in the Orient," *Korea Mission Field*, Vol. 21, No. 2, February 1925.

"Posture in the Preservation of the Perineum," *China Medical Journal*, September 1927.

"The Women's Medical Training Institute," *Korea Mission Field*, Vol. 24, No. 9, September 1928.

"The Double Cross Seal and the New Year in Korea," The Liberty (New York) Gazette, December 29, 1938.

"A Romantic Leap Year Party," The Liberty Register, June 6, 1940.

"Friendly Cooperation Between China, Japan, Manchuria, and Korea," Liberty Ad-Viser, Sullivan County Press, Thursday, November 6, 1941.

"Foreign Medical Women in Korea," *Journal of the American Medical Women's Association*, Vol. 5, October 1950, 404-405.

Index